SERIOUSLY FROM SCRATCH

HOW TO COOK THE MOST DELICIOUS FOOD EVER BY MAKING EVERY SINGLE COMPONENT YOURSELF

JOE GATTO

PROFESSIONAL CHEF
WRITER OF THE AWARD-WINNING FILM *OVERSERVED*

First published in 2016 by
Page Street Publishing Co.
27 Congress Street, Suite 103
Salem, MA 01970
www.pagestreetpublishing.com

Distributed by Macmillan, sales in Canada by The Canadian Manda Group.

19 18 17 16 1 2 3 4 5

ISBN-13: 978-1-62414-310-6
ISBN-10: 1-62414-310-5

Library of Congress Control Number: 2015960282

Cover and book design by Page Street Publishing Co.
Photography by Ken Goodman

Printed and bound in China

Page Street is proud to be a member of 1% for the Planet. Members donate one percent of their sales to one or more of the over 1,500 environmental and sustainability charities across the globe who participate in this program.

THIS BOOK IS DEDICATED TO EVERYONE WHO
HAS BIG DREAMS...AND TO SNOOP DOGG BECAUSE
SNOOP DOGG IS AWESOME.

CONTENTS

FROM SCRATCH

HOW WE PLANTED A SEED AND EVERYTHING GREW

Do you want to have fun in the kitchen? Do you want to make dishes that make people punch themselves in the face they are so amazing? Do you want to release that creative, culinary genius lurking deep inside your soul? Well, you have made the right choice in picking up this book. I know. Trust me. I know. I've heard it all. "From scratch?! Are you insane?" "It takes much too long." "It's way too hard." "No way, Joe—are you some type of crazy person?" I'm here to tell you that it's all a pack of lies. Well, maybe not the "crazy person" part, but everything else is greatly exaggerated. You can do this! It is super fun and you only need one tool to do it. That's right—one tool. Passion. Not a cool knife, not a fancy pan. Those things help, but without passion, you're trying to kill a grizzly with a BB gun. Dalí wasn't a genius because he had a good brush.

My journey did not start where you think it did. Like life, it is a long, winding road, always fluctuating and shifting. Becoming a chef with a cutting-edge cooking show has been an amalgamation of experiences: rewarding, frustrating and also the greatest times of my life. I want to share my experiences with you. This isn't your typical cookbook, trust me. We are going to take a journey together into food and its spirit. I'm going to teach you knife skills so your confidence in the kitchen will soar, and I'll show you how to sear, grind and caramelize. But that's just the tip of the iceberg. We're going to start from the ground up, so you will understand food from its fundamental beginnings, and we are going to have a blast doing it! I don't want you to buy this book just for the recipes. This is my story, my life and why I have such an appetite for food, community and family. Food is the gateway to happiness. It's not just a line; I truly believe that. After you read this book, I know you will, too!

If you've ever seen my show, you know I love to get to the bottom of things. If we are going to use salt, I want to be pulling it out of the Atlantic Ocean and making my own. Cheese? I'm milking cows. Charcoal—yep, let's make some carbon! Why? Because I think that is the best way to figure out how to make whatever you want. To understand how things work is integral to becoming a confident cook in the kitchen. You don't have to be trained in the culinary arts to make rock star food.

I grew up in my mom's kitchen, and the fantastic memories still make me smile and feel like Brie—gooey all over. Sitting on the counter as a kid tasked to the small jobs, sifting and stirring, and then being promoted to the big time, where I was chopping and sautéing. I found my love of food and family right there. It's also where I honed my gift of gab. My mom, Lorraine, was and still is always cooking, amazing smells wafting through the house like some unseen poltergeist of yumminess. I was always hungry and there was always something delectable waiting in the fridge, from homemade deep-dish pizza to roasted potatoes to butterscotch pudding and everything in between. This gene of culinary obsession has been passed on to my two munchkins, Benjamin and Cassidy. Now my little sous chefs are up on my counter pulling fresh mozzarella, cranking pastas, stuffing empanadas and so much more. I find this time to be a wonderful time to connect; the kids are so much more open to telling me about their day as we're cooking together. They openly share things I don't think they would tell me if I just asked. Nothing bad, mind you, but hilarious stories of their youthful days. Who their best friends are, how much they love puddles or our cats, Ripley and Zen. Because as you're cooking, the conversation flows.

They call the kitchen the heart of the house for a reason. It's where memories are created. I know at every party or family gathering everyone congregates in the kitchen. A culinary church that has lots of dedicated parishioners. I rejoice in the laughter and stories that flow, as well as some great drinks, as everyone works in harmony to create a meal. But I'm getting ahead of myself. Let me start at the beginning of how I became a chef and started my own radical cooking show.

My path into the culinary world really started off in an unexpected place: Hollywood, California, when I was an independent filmmaker. I know, it sounds like the start of a movie, right? So there I was, a wide-eyed twenty-year-old with my whole life ahead of me. The left coast had intrigued me since I was a kid; I was obsessed with cinema and the craft of filmmaking. So bypassing the college route, I hopped on a plane and landed in northern California, ready to become the next De Niro. I landed a couple of small roles in independent features and music videos. It was like a drug, and I was hooked. The whole time I was cooking from scratch like I always had. Little did I know down the line of life both obsessions would collide.

I took a job in a small production company and soon made a great friend: Larry Sara, who, like me, was obsessed with film. We had endless discussions over which director had the best visuals and what the funniest movie of all time was. *Monty Python and the Holy Grail*? "I cut your arm off. No you didn't. What's that, then? 'Tis just a flesh wound." Soon we were making our own films and music videos and having boundless amounts of fun. Food always played an integral part of it. Wrap parties inevitably ended up at my house with me at the stove, regaling our successes and failures of the past shoot over a fresh plate of pasta and marinara. These were fantastic times, even if the films were not instant classics.

After eight years, Massachusetts beckoned my return, and next thing I knew, I was shoveling again. I continued making films and got my first feature up and running, called *Overserved*, a scathing comedy about working in a wild restaurant. Food again was always playing a huge role, with me cooking for rehearsals or production meetings. I met some people who would become lifelong friends when we filmed at the Sam Adams brewery every weekend during the summer of 2003. Shooting fifteen-hour days, we poured our hearts and souls into every detail. We sweated every line and then flocked to the large, family-style picnic table to empty the kegs as we talked about all that went wrong and right and how much we had ahead. I laughed until my sides hurt every night, woke up exhausted and couldn't wait for more.

This is also where I met the most significant person in my life, my stunning wife, Carey. I was looking for an assistant director and she came highly recommended by one of my best friends and cinematographer, Tony Flanagan. At our first meeting I was impressed by her go-get-it attitude. She wanted to make movies and she was determined. She was smart, driven and beautiful, and I hired her within minutes. We fit like peanut butter and jelly. She soon rose to the title of producer, and the film was running like clockwork. The summer flew by and the film was done while Carey completed her master's degree in film at Emerson College. We put *Overserved* into the festival circuit, watched it pick up some awards and showed it at local theaters. We had the time of our lives. Carey and I continued to work together, making music videos and short films and writing scripts. A romance blossomed; we were smitten and still are.

Carey and I worked long and hard at our film career, with me always cooking for her, trying to impress her more each time I whipped up a dish. She loved my food, and my culinary prowess was growing. We got hitched and disembarked to LA because that's where you go if movies are your craving. I was going back to Cali, Cali and I was pumped! We arrived in the City of Angels and hit the ground running, making short films and writing scripts. Pitching and connecting. We were really putting the pedal to the metal, but something was different. I was changing. Like a lycanthrope caught in the grasp of a full moon. I felt it to the core of my being.

I had unconsciously stopped reading film books and started voraciously consuming cookbooks. The culinary arts were beckoning me. I still loved film, but it was losing the battle to my obsession with food and from-scratch cooking. When Carey then divulged a little secret—that she was pregnant with our first tater tot—it was the tipping point. I chatted with Carey and told her cooking was my path and I knew it. She knew it as well. Next thing you know, I was teaching cooking classes out of our condo in Westchester and each week more students would appear. Like a Fabergé shampoo commercial from the '70s, it seemed that everyone was telling two friends. Soon our condo was bustling with home cooks of all skill levels with the desire to up their gastronomic game. I had found my calling. Teaching was my nirvana.

It was on like Donkey Kong. We wanted to be near our family now that we had our first child, so we sold our condo and headed back to the East Coast. Carey, after successfully selling our home, decided she had a future in real estate. She was right. Boston was the perfect choice. I started teaching and loved it; I found I had a real knack for connecting with people and making cooking accessible and enjoyable. Through teaching I got hired as a private chef by a local company and started cooking for families every week. I couldn't believe how much fun I was having and how quickly it was all happening.

One night Carey and I were up, having a few adult beverages, listening to Snoop, just enjoying life. We started talking about cooking shows that were on and how we would do one. Time flew, drinks tipped and next thing we knew, the seed of an idea had been planted. *From Scratch* was sprouting. I sat down the next day with a large latte glued to my hand and commenced to write feverishly. I knew I wanted to make a show that was really distinctive, got to the core of food and explored the stories behind everything in the kitchen. I called in every favor I had in the production world and three months later, we were shooting the pilot. Old friends from *Overserved* came on board. Tony behind the lens, Shane Bronson handling sound and Carey at the producing helm. I decided to make an all-time favorite of mine, a BLT, but all from scratch. That meant breaking down a whole hog, pulling out the belly and curing and smoking it to make our own bacon. I made the bread and the mayo and even visited a local farm to source the tomatoes. My good chum Ryan Kavanaugh served as editor, comedian Todd Gorell did some riotous bits dressed as a strip of bacon and we got cooking! Once we saw the first cut, we knew we had something delicious.

The other from-scratch project we had been working on also was born, my gorgeous daughter, Cassidy. Life was kicking into fifth gear, almost overwhelming, but then I recalled what Ferris Bueller said: "Life moves pretty fast. If you don't stop and look around once in a while, you could miss it." I stood back, inhaled, reveled in the craziness and excitement and jumped back in with both feet. We instantaneously dove into production on the second show, with Ryan directing, and added multifaceted cameraman Adam Mikaelian. We ground flour to make pasta and milked cows to make butter and cheese. Both kids came on and the camera ate them up. We were sizzling. It was then that Carey asked me if I would do a special from-scratch class as a thank-you to people she worked closely with in real estate. Of course, I said I would love to. Who knew that moment would be one of the most important decisions of my life?

The class was a blast and Carey's colleagues were amazing people. After the class wrapped, we were all chatting and enjoying a cocktail. It turned out that they were all part of an angels investor group. I told them about the show and they were intrigued. They wanted a meeting. Carey and I were prepared; we pitched our idea for a whole season and for merchandising, Shark Tank–style. We had designed a sizzle reel for this very purpose, and that put us over the top. Negotiations began; contacts were put in place and boom shakalaka—we had a show! We were over the moon that we were funded for an entire season. Joy. Tears. WORK. We assembled our go-to team and added some crucial folks: Emmy Fay; our new production manager; Emily, the greatest assistant known to man; and I finally got some killer kitchen help with Jonah, Phil and my mom! Yep, if there's going to be cooking going on, then I want my mom there to make sure it's rocking and rolling. She's superlative!

Once we designed the season we looked at it as a whole, laughing and crying at how ambitious it was. We were going to be doing things I never even imagined. Traveling across New England to hand-forge knives, make charcoal, distill rum, cure charcuterie and so much more. I was salivating to get started. We decided to shoot all the kitchen parts first. So it was recipe-writing time and, oh man, when you have a show called *From Scratch*, there can't be any cans or boxes on set. You have to make everything! It was a challenge, and recipe testing was arduous and delicious all at the same time. The creative juices were flowing and I wanted to push the food and the format of the show as far as possible. Carey, Kav and I worked away on the scripts as we also set up the merchandise side of the business. Looking back on it, I can't believe we got it done. It was a crazy amount of work, but we killed it! I have never laughed that much in my whole life. Carey and I were with people we loved in an egoless atmosphere, creating cutting-edge art together. The kids became regulars and were adorable. The kitchen was wrapped, but it was just the tip of the carbon steel knife. Thirty-plus location shoots loomed in the distance. Taunting us. Challenging us. Bring it.

It was going to be a slugfest and we knew we could take a punch. We took the locations head-on. The summer was a whirlwind. One day we're doing an authentic clam bake, crack of dawn the next morn I'm driving a lobster boat! Then I'm at Fenway Park shooting on their mind-blowing rooftop garden and then suddenly crafting rum at a distillery! I really feel blessed to have all of this happening and doing it with my family and friends. As I write this, we are wrapping up and editing. I'm on pins and needles every day, as footage flows in. I hope you tune in: It's going to be a wild ride. The roller coaster is cresting. Arms up!

Joe Gatto

Chef Joe Gatto

BURGERS, BUNS AND BACON! OH MY!

One of the things that always hits the spot for me is a good old-fashioned burger. Hot and juicy with melted cheese, bacon, fresh onion and a side of crispy fries ... oh yeah, heaven. I have tremendous memories of being a youngster and asking my mom what's for dinner and she would say burgers and fries. PUMPED. I was constantly early to the counter on those nights, trying to sneak a lava-hot fry seconds out of its oil Jacuzzi. It's something I always order when I'm out, no matter the place. I think the sign of a great place can be judged on the quality of its burger.

When I set out to make a from-scratch burger I knew the recipe testing was going to be a ton of fun. Boy, was I right. I was in heaven. It was then I knew why Wimpy was always trying to get cash off Popeye to buy one. So in my quest for the Holy Grail I stumbled across a few musts. Homemade bun, no exceptions. Condiments and pickles—make 'em. You don't buy a Ferrari and put cloth seats in it, right? As far as the meat, chuck and sirloin were working for me very well, but I felt there was a band member missing. Brisket got a try out but was a little tone deaf. Short rib was too much of a diva. I was perplexed. Then I did something outrageous. I had some homemade bacon in my fridge because I always do and I ground that up with the chuck and sirloin. My band was a colossal hit. I mean #1 hits across the board!

I could not believe the depth of flavor this combo achieved. I was in burger meat nirvana. I had done what I set out to do, but what kind of rock band doesn't have groupies? My burger was no exception. Fries. I needed fries, but not any fry would do. Parmesan herb fries started to follow my burger band religiously. Now come on everyone, let's go see them in concert and get this party started!

BEST BURGERS EVAH

I was literally stopped in the streets in Boston and told, "I had one of your burgers at the farmers' market last week and it was the best f#@king burger I've ever had. I've been dreaming about it." Dropping the mic and walking away. Make these and please bring me one. Please.

MAPLE CHIPOTLE BACON (AKA PORKY LOVE)

BACON!!!!! We are going to use this in our burger grind to take it into the stratosphere! This is not store-bought, flavorless, saline-injected bacon. This is the real stuff. Savory, sweet, smoky and packed full of flavor. Trust me, the difference is huge. I love making BLTs with this bacon.

PREP TIME: 30 MINUTES

CURING TIME: 8 DAYS

START THIS PROCESS 9 DAYS BEFORE CREATING THE BEST BURGER EVAH

YIELD: 5 POUNDS (2275 G)

- 2 oz (56 g) kosher salt (weigh this)
- 2 tsp (10 g) pink salt
- ½ cup (100 g) sugar
- 1 tbsp (9 g) roasted garlic powder
- 1 tbsp (7 g) smoked paprika
- 1 tbsp (15 ml) molasses
- 2 tbsp (30 ml) honey
- ½ cup (120 ml) maple syrup
- ½ cup (50 g) roasted garlic
- 6 chipotles in adobo, chopped
- 5 lb (2250 g) pork belly
- 2 (2-gallon [8-L]) zip-top bags

Combine the salts, sugar, garlic powder, paprika, molasses, honey, maple syrup, roasted garlic and chipotles in a large bowl. I like to place the pork belly on a baking sheet to cut down on the mess. Working clean is very important. It does get a bit messy, so set up for success. Have paper towels ready and give yourself room to work before you start. Also, clear a space where you will be putting it in the fridge now. I'll wait.

Rub the cure all over the belly; make sure you get really good coverage. Leave no pork belly showing. Place the pork belly in a large 2-gallon (8-L) zip-top bag. This is a little tricky, so if you have someone around who doesn't mind touching pork belly, recruit them. Close the bag, squeezing out all the air. Place that bag inside the second zip-top bag and close that bag. I use two bags because once I used only one bag and it leaked all over the fridge. Can you say big-time bummer? It's a precaution, but one I strongly suggest. Now put it in the fridge on the bottom shelf. It's going to hang out there for 8 days. Each day, flip the bag over. Yes, it's a commitment, but one you will be glad you made. You will see liquid will begin to fill the bag. That's a good thing; the cure is happening.

After 8 days, it should be done. Nice and firm. Wash the cure off the meat, rinsing thoroughly. Using paper towels, pat the bacon really dry and set it on a rack over a baking sheet. Some people air-dry it in the fridge overnight. I don't: I want bacon! Just make sure it's dried really well.

FROM-SCRATCH SECRET
IT'S A CARBON PARTY! LUMP CHARCOAL FROM SCRATCH!

Making charcoal at home sounds crazy, but what's cooler than to say you made your own charcoal? Nothing! It's surprisingly not difficult, once you have the proper equipment to do it. I learned to make charcoal from Bob Wells, who runs a company called Bio-Char. Make sure you are doing this in a safe place to light a large fire. Not near your house or on your newly manicured lawn. Find a good open space, and you're going to need to leave it for a while, so think about that as well. One of the cool things I learned is that whatever biomass you put in comes out as carbon. So if you put in a flower, it comes out looking like a charcoal flower. You put in a dead chipmunk. Guess what? Dead charcoal chipmunk. So cool. A boy will always be a boy.

PREP TIME: 1 HOUR

COOK TIME: 1 DAY

YIELD: 20 POUNDS (9100 G)

1 clean 55-gallon (200-L) metal drum

1 clean 30-gallon (120-L) metal drum with lid

Huge stack of dry sticks, any size

55-gallon (200-L) drum lid with 4-foot (120-cm) chimney welded onto the center

Something to light a fire

Start with a 55-gallon (200-L) drum with eight 1-inch (2.5-cm) holes drilled around the side of the barrel 8 inches (20 cm) from the bottom and 6 secondary air holes around the top of the drum. The 30-gallon (120-L) drum slips inside. The 30-gallon (120-L) drum needs to have about six ½-inch (1.3-cm) holes drilled through the bottom for air to pass. It is the retort chamber. Place the small drum inside the large drum and fill it with dry hardwood. You can use sticks of old lumber as long as it's never been treated with anything and has no nails in it. Now place the lid on the inner barrel. Now you need to fill in the spaces around the small drum. Wood should be surrounding it. Pack it tightly, and then cover the top of the small drum with wood as well. Think of it as cooking the wood inside the small drum and the large drum is the oven. The gasses get cooked out of the wood and deny oxygen to it. That way, it doesn't burn the wood and turn it to ash. The volatiles get cooked out of the wood as well, like the water. Now light the wood surrounding the small drum. Get it going really well and then put on the lid with the chimney, which creates the thermal syphon. Once it's lit you can walk away. It will take care of itself. Bob calls it the "light it and leave it" system. Then the next day, when it's completely cool, you dump water all over it to make sure there is no fire left. Finished charcoal that is done correctly should be cooked all the way through. No brown inside and it should not have ash. It's official: you just made carbon! Whoa, you're awesome!

LET'S GET SMOKING!

Lump charcoal
A chimney starter
Smoker
Water or beer
Temperature probe
Applewood and hickory chunks, soaked

Dump your lump charcoal into your chimney starter and light them. Get them super hot. When they are hot, pour them into a smoker over more lump charcoal. Let the lump heat up and you get a constant temperature; I like it at 225°F (105°C). Fill the water pan with water or beer. Place an internal probe into the bacon so you can keep an eye on the temperature. (Insert the probe from the side, not the top.) Add the soaked wood chunks and let them begin to smoke. Place the pork belly, skin-side down, in the smoker and smoke. The time varies, but it is usually around 4 hours for me. The key is an internal temperature of 150°F (66°C). Once it hits 150°F (66°C), take it out!

While still warm, remove the skin from the bottom of the bacon. Just slide your knife between the skin and the bacon and remove it. (Save it to flavor soups or make chicharones for a Pats' game.) Let the bacon cool and slice by hand, or if you have access to a deli slicer, use that. That's it—now you have your own bacon! Use it how you see fit. I say fry some up ASAP and eat it, but that's just me. It will stay fresh for up to 1 week but not a shot in hell it lasts that long. Be sure to keep some to make the burger grind!

KILLER KETCHUP

Homemade ketchup? Really, Joe? Now you've gone too far. But wait, hear me out. Once you try this, you will be astounded at the deep flavors. I add chipotles to this for a little kick! This is not your parents' ketchup. No preservatives, no dyes. Just from-scratch yumminess.

PREP TIME: 20 MINUTES

COOK TIME: 1 HOUR

MAKE THIS 2 DAYS BEFORE CREATING THE BEST BURGER EVAH

YIELD: 3–4 CUPS (720–960 G)

- 2 tbsp (30 ml) canola oil
- 1 large onion, chopped
- 6 cloves garlic, chopped
- 1 tsp (3 g) mustard powder
- 1 tsp (2 g) celery salt
- 2 tbsp (30 g) chipotles in adobo sauce
- ½ tsp smoked paprika
- ½ tsp ground allspice
- ½ tsp black pepper
- 1 tsp (5 g) salt
- 4 cups (600 g) skinned, chopped fresh tomatoes
- 2 tbsp (24 g) tomato paste
- ½ cup (90 g) dark brown sugar, packed
- ¼ cup (60 ml) cider vinegar
- ¼ cup (60 ml) champagne vinegar

In a large Dutch oven, heat the oil over medium heat, add the onion and sauté for 5 minutes, then add the garlic and sauté for 5 minutes more. Stir constantly. Add the mustard powder, celery salt, chipotles, paprika, allspice, pepper and salt and cook for 2 minutes, stirring constantly.

Add your tomatoes, tomato paste, brown sugar and vinegars and then simmer, uncovered, for 1 hour, stirring frequently. You have to be careful that it doesn't burn, so make sure you are stirring. Use an immersion blender and blend it until it's smooth. When it's cool, place into mason jars and let it sit in your fridge overnight. The next day, make a burger, put the ketchup on and smile wide.

PATRICIA BRAGG
N.D. Ph.D.
BRAGG
Established 1912
ORGANIC
RAW ~ UNFILTERED
APPLE CIDER
VINEGAR
With The 'Mother'
USDA ORGANIC
UNPASTEURIZED
Naturally Gluten Free
16 FL OZ ~ 473 mL
Serving Health Worldwide Since 1912
Made from Organic Apples
16,9 fl. oz. (500ml)
FSC CERTIFIED
100%

PATRICIA BRAGG
BRAGG
ORGANIC
RAW ~ UNFILTERED
APPLE CIDER
VINEGAR
With The 'Mother'
UNPASTEURIZED
Naturally Gluten Free
16 FL OZ ~ 473 mL
Serving Health Worldwide Since 1912

FIERY AND ZESTY MUSTARD

I'm a big mustard fan, especially when it's got some heat to it. This mustard is all that and more. Zesty, with some real heat, it will make any burger, sandwich, dog or wrap come alive. It's also a great thing to add to a homemade dressing to give it that little kick! We'll use it to make the perfect burger sauce in a few pages.

PREP TIME: 20 MINUTES

MAKE THIS 2 DAYS BEFORE CREATING THE BEST BURGER EVAH

YIELD: 1–1½ CUPS (240–360 G)

4 tbsp (44 g) yellow mustard seeds

3 tbsp (33 g) brown mustard seeds

¼ cup (36 g) spicy mustard powder

2 cloves garlic, minced

½ cup (120 ml) apple cider vinegar

1 tbsp (12 g) freshly ground horseradish

2 tsp (10 ml) honey

1 tsp (5 g) kosher salt

¼ cup (60 ml) water

2 tbsp (30 ml) dark beer

Grind the mustard seeds in a spice grinder. Pour into a bowl, add the spicy mustard powder and stir together. Add the garlic, vinegar, horseradish, honey and salt. Stir to combine. Add the water and beer and use an immersion blender to blend for 1 minute.

Place into the fridge overnight. The next day the mustard will be good to go! YUM!

MAYO THAT ROCKS

Homemade mayo is just one of those things that everyone should make, it's so easy. The mayo is so creamy, fresh and delicious. Plus, once you make it, the things you can add to it are endless. Spicy sriracha mayo, lime mayo, fresh herb mayo and on and on and on! This uses raw egg, so I wouldn't feed it to children or pregnant women. Just to be safe! This it the second component of our bomb burger sauce coming up next.

PREP TIME: 15 MINUTES

MAKE THIS 2 DAYS BEFORE CREATING THE BEST BURGER EVAH

YIELD: 1 CUP (240 G)

1 egg yolk

1 tsp (5 g) Fiery and Zesty Mustard (page 25)

1 tbsp (15 ml) white vinegar

1 cup (240 ml) canola oil, divided

In your blender, add the egg yolk, mustard, vinegar and ¼ cup (60 ml) of the oil. Blend for 30 seconds until combined. Turn it off and quickly scrape down the sides. Turn the blender back on, and while it's running, slowly drizzle in the remaining ¾ cup (180 ml) oil. Blend until, well, until it looks like mayo! Once it does, it's good to go! Refrigerate it.

crafted for quality–
sealed for freshness™
Made in USA
Ball®

B'S BURGER SAUCE

By putting in all that from-scratch work, we create a burger sauce that is killer. I love this sauce on my burgers and dogs, but don't stop there—dip fries in it, spread it on a wrap, the uses are endless! It's called B's Burger Sauce because that's my nickname for my son, Benjamin, and he's awesome.

PREP TIME: 5 MINUTES

MAKE THIS 2 DAYS BEFORE CREATING THE BEST BURGER EVAH

YIELD: 1¼ CUPS (300 G)

½ cup (120 g) Killer Ketchup (page 22)

½ cup (120 g) Mayo That Rocks (page 26)

¼ cup (60 g) Fiery and Zesty Mustard (page 25)

Mix all the ingredients together in a bowl. Make a day ahead to let the flavors blend. Slather on burgers or dogs.

BODACIOUS BEER HAMBURGER BUNS

Well, after all that work to make our own burger grind, we can't just "chuck" it onto a store-bought bun all willy-nilly! We need a roll that's going to stand up and be noticed. Fluffy and flavorful, this bun is a superstar. Let cool and store in zip-top bags.

PREP TIME: 2 HOURS

COOK TIME: 12–15 MINUTES

MAKE THESE THE DAY BEFORE CREATING THE BEST BURGER EVAH

YIELD: 8 BUNS

12 oz (360 ml) good pale ale, at room temperature

1 tbsp (11 g) light brown sugar

2¼ tsp (9 g) active dry yeast

¼ cup (60 g) butter, melted

1 tsp (5 g) kosher salt

3–4 cups (360–480 g) all-purpose flour, or more as needed

1 egg, beaten with 1 tbsp (15 ml) water

In a large bowl, add the beer and dissolve the sugar in it. Add the yeast and let it bloom, about 10 minutes. It's not going to be a huge bloom but that's okay. Don't panic. Stir in the butter and salt. Then add the flour 1 cup (120 g) at a time until the dough is not sticky. Once it's all incorporated, turn the dough out onto a lightly floured counter and knead for about 5 minutes, until the dough is smooth. If it's still tacky, add a little flour, 1 tablespoon (12 g) at a time.

Place the dough in a lightly oiled bowl, cover the bowl with a dishtowel and place in a warm area of the kitchen for an hour and let it do its thing.

When the dough has doubled in size, take it out of the bowl and divide it into 8 equal pieces about 4 ounces (112 g) each. Shape each piece into a ball and place the balls 2 inches (5 cm) apart on a baking sheet lined with parchment paper. Now they need to rise again, so cover them with a towel and let them rise for 30 minutes. Preheat your oven to 400°F (200°C, or gas mark 6).

After 30 minutes, remove the towel and brush them with the egg wash. Pop them in the oven and bake for 12–15 minutes. They should be golden brown. Let them cool and start making some awesome burgers!

HARPOON
TAKE 5

BEST BURGERS EVAH

Whether these come off the grill or out of a cast-iron pan, once you take your first juicy bite and all the rich flavors from bacon to chuck punch your taste buds in the face, you will never buy a store-bought grind again.

PREP TIME: 1 HOUR

COOK TIME: 10 MINUTES

IT'S HERE! BURGER-FEST TIME!

YIELD: 15–20 BURGERS

3 lb (1350 g) chuck

1 lb (450 g) boneless sirloin

1 lb (450 g) Maple Chipotle Bacon (page 17)

4 tbsp (40 g) roughly chopped garlic

Bodacious Beer Hamburger Buns (page 30)

B's Burger Sauce (page 29), for serving

Lettuce, for topping

Tomato, for topping

Now, grinding your own meat is satisfying and really easy. There are just a couple of things you want to make sure you do to make it safe and easy.

Take all your meat and freeze it for about an hour. You don't want it rock solid but firm enough so it cubes easily. Cut all your meat into 1- to 2-inch (2.5- to 5-cm) cubes and throw it back in the freezer, along with your grinding tools, for 30 minutes as you make space to grind your awesome new burgers.

Get a big bowl, a really big bowl, and place it under your grinder. Take the cubed meat and begin grinding with the ¼-inch (6-mm) die, alternating between cuts and garlic. Now you want to move fast here. If things start to get warm, that's not good. The fat will smear and your burgers will be gritty. Not cool. So remember, cool and fast. Just like James Dean. Now, when it's all ground, you can form your patties!

MAKE THE FRIES NOW!!! JUST BEFORE THE BURGERS GO ON!!!!

Time to cook those delicious burgers. Preheat your grill for at least 15 minutes. Place the burgers on the grill and do not move them (no touching!) for 5 minutes, then flip to the clean part of the grill. You want a nice char. Let them cook on the second side for about 4 minutes. Take off the grill and let them rest for 3 to 5 minutes.

Thick, thin, flat-top or grill, loaded with toppings or naked as a jaybird, these are can't-miss burgers! For me, I'm grabbing one of our bodacious burger rolls, spreading on burger sauce, slapping my best burger evah on it and topping it with fresh lettuce, tomato and going to town. Of course, with a big plate of Parmesan Herb Fries (page 34) on the side!

PARMESAN HERB FRIES

Who doesn't love a crispy French fry? If you don't, you are suspect in my mind. The double fry technique we use here is a great way to get the fries perfectly crisp. Use whatever herbs you like or make a spice sprinkle for them! They are a blank canvas. Paint away. My son Benjamin swears these are the "Greatest fries in the whole world; seriously, Dad, the greatest!"

PREP TIME: 30 MINUTES

COOK TIME: 15 MINUTES

MAKE THESE THE DAY OF THE ULTIMATE BURGER FEST

YIELD: 4 GENEROUS SERVINGS

3 (8-oz [227-g]) russet potatoes, washed but not peeled

½ cup (45 g) freshly grated Parmesan

2 cloves garlic, minced

1 tsp (2 g) minced fresh rosemary

1 tsp (2 g) minced fresh oregano

½ tsp salt

⅛ tsp cayenne pepper

2 qt (1.9 L) canola or any neutral oil

Here you are julienning the potatoes. I like doing it by hand; it takes some practice, but doesn't everything that's worthwhile?

Slice the potatoes into 1-inch (2.5-cm) thick planks and cut each plank into ½-inch (1.3-cm) wide bars. Add to a bowl of cold water as they are cut so they release starch. Continue until all the potatoes are julienned. If this is confusing, just slice them into a shape that looks like a French fry. Change the water and soak for 10 minutes. This helps make the fries crispy. Lay out on paper towels to dry. Blot them completely dry. A wet potato will splatter you with hot oil and make you sad.

Combine the Parmesan, garlic, herbs, salt and cayenne in a bowl and set aside.

In a large Dutch oven, heat the oil to 300°F (150°C). Make sure the oil is no more than halfway up the sides or it will overflow and you will have a big fire and not be happy! Fry the potatoes, in handful-size batches, until blond and limp, moving them around so they don't stick, 4–5 minutes. Remember, we are cooking these twice. This step we are not crisping, we are just cooking the potato until it's limp. Remove, drain on paper towels and bring the heat up to 350°F (177°C). Refry until crisp, 3–4 minutes. Once they are nice and crispy, remove them to a paper towel–lined stainless bowl, sprinkle with the Parmesan mix immediately, remove the paper towel and toss until coated. Serve and receive praise.

from scratch
Chef Joe Gatto

LET'S HIT THE DELI!

Delis are a shrine for me. I love to pray at the altar of smoked and cured meats as often as I can. In other words, eat, eat and eat some more. I seriously adore all deli foods, from the addicting potato knish to the delectable cheese blintzes. Matzo ball soup has true healing power. But for me, it's the Rueben. I am infatuated. It's the greatest deli sandwich ever created—tender corned beef, tangy Russian dressing, crunchy coleslaw and gooey Swiss cheese. And let's not forget the butter and toasted rye bread. Drooling.

I am a self-proclaimed Rueben freak. There might have been an intervention at one point. Maybe. So if I was going to make my own, you know I had to go all the way. This means that I would have to tackle pastrami from its humble beginnings. Just thinking about the chance to make my very own corned beef from tip to tail was exhilarating. Maybe I'll make it spicy! Maybe I'll cure it longer! I couldn't stop. My head was spinning. It was on. Oh yeah, it was on. Big time.

I finished my voyage. The Rueben sat in front of me. Almost taunting me. Saying, "I dare you to eat me." Was I worth it? I reached out and picked up this slice of paradise. I took a bite. I'd love to describe what happened here but I think I blacked out. It was that incredible. All the work was worth it. I'm going to show you to make it all, from corned beef to pickles. So let's jump in with both feet and get started. I'm also going to take you for a stroll down Pastrami Lane, corned beef's peppery sibling. It's another beloved deli meat of mine—it's tender, spicy and smoky. Love it with just some phenomenal bread and zesty mustard. Enough talk; now let's go church up!

THE CORNED BEEF REUBEN

Building the perfect Reuben is an art form. The wait is over. Let's do this!

SAUERKRAUT (HARD TO SPELL, YUMMY TO EAT!)

I'll be honest: I never liked sauerkraut, not one bit. Until I made it, then I got it. Crunchy with that gentle tangy finish, it's perfect to help balance a rich sandwich like the Reuben. Plus, you get to ferment, which is really cool!

PREP TIME: 20 MINUTES

COOK/FERMENT TIME: 30 DAYS

START THIS A MONTH BEFORE CREATING THE REUBEN

YIELD: 2 QUARTS (1.8 L)

2 (1-qt [1-L]) mason jars
1 large head cabbage
2 tbsp (36 g) sea salt
1 tbsp (11 g) caraway seeds
2 pieces cheesecloth

Make sure your mason jars are very clean. I like to run them through the dishwasher once before using them. Clean hands as well!

Remove the tattered, browning leaves on the outside of the cabbage, if there are any. Reserve 2 large leaves for later. Slice the cabbage head into quarters, and at a 45-degree angle, remove the core and discard. Now slice the cabbage into thin strips about ¼-inch (6-mm) thick. Place it all into a bowl and sprinkle the salt over the top. Let it sit for 15 minutes, because the salt needs to do its thing. Now comes the fun part: you need to squeeze and crush the cabbage. It will become limp after about 5 minutes. You will see liquid gathering at the bottom. This is excellent. Now leave it for 30 minutes on the counter to do its thing. After 30 minutes, stir in the caraway seeds.

Now start packing the cabbage into the mason jars. Pack it tight and leave 3 inches (7.6 cm) of space from the top. Pour in the extra liquid from the bowl and fill it to 1 inch (2.5 cm) from the top. Press the cabbage down so it is completely submerged under the liquid. If there isn't enough liquid, make a simple brine of ½ tablespoon (9 g) salt to 2 cups (475 ml) water and use that. Tap the jar lightly on the counter to remove any bubbles.

(continued)

SAUERKRAUT (CONTINUED)

Take the reserved cabbage leaves and stuff them into the jars to help keep the cabbage pressed down. Now cover it with the cheesecloth and secure it with a rubber band. It needs to sit on the counter for a month at a temperature between 65°F and 70°F (18°C and 21°C). Also, don't let it sit in the sun. No bueno. Pack it down once a day for the first week so it stays submerged. The next thing you know, the fermentation process will start rocking, small bubbles will start forming and a white foam will collect on the surface—this is all good stuff. If any brown scum develops, just skim it off. No worries. I like to try it after the first week to see how it's doing. I like it after 3 weeks, but you decide how you like it. The flavor changes the longer it ferments. When it gets to where you like it, place it in the fridge to stop the fermentation process. Now go make that Reuben.

PICKLING SPICE

One of the keys to making great corned beef and pastrami is the pickling spice. I love this one. Tons of flavor with a little kick. This makes enough for both the corned beef and the pastrami.

PREP TIME: 20 MINUTES

MAKE THIS 10 DAYS BEFORE CREATING THE REUBEN OR PASTRAMI SANDWICH

YIELD: ABOUT ½ CUP (95 G)

3 tbsp (15 g) whole black peppercorns

6 bay leaves

1 Ceylon cinnamon stick, crumbled

2-inch (5-cm) piece fresh ginger, peeled

3 cloves garlic, smashed

2 tbsp (12 g) coriander seeds

1 tbsp (4 g) red pepper flakes

1 tbsp (11 g) brown mustard seeds

1 tbsp (11 g) yellow mustard seeds

½ tbsp (3 g) whole allspice berries

2 tsp (4 g) dill seeds

1 tsp (2 g) fennel seed

1 tsp (2 g) cumin seed

1 tsp (2 g) whole cloves

1 tsp (2 g) annatto seeds

Combine all the ingredients in a bowl. Store in a sealed container.

KICK-ASS CORNED BEEF

The cool thing I learned while making from-scratch corned beef and pastrami was that the only difference between the two is corned beef is just steamed and pastrami is rubbed, smoked and steamed. The only other difference is you trim all the fat before you cure the corned beef because the fat will be chewy and rubbery when we steam it, while with the pastrami you lightly trim it because the fat gets all yummy when it smokes. The pickling spice and cure time are the same. So what I like to do is get two 8-pound (3600-g) briskets and trim one really well for corned beef and lightly trim the other for pastrami and cure/pickle them both at the same time! I find it's so much easier to do both of them at once. Then you will have more awesome meats to choose from! Now let's go make some yumminess!

PREP TIME: 45 MINUTES

CURE TIME: 9 DAYS

MAKE THIS 9 DAYS BEFORE CREATING THE REUBEN

YIELD: 8–10 SERVINGS

1 gallon (3.8 L) water

¼ cup (47 g) Pickling Spice (page 43)

½ cup (90 g) brown sugar

¼ cup (60 ml) maple syrup

1 cup (288 g) kosher salt

2 tsp (10 g) Prague powder #1 (you can find this on Amazon—it's worth it)

8-lb (3600-g) beef brisket

4 (2-gallon [8-L]) zip-top bags

Place the water, pickling spice, brown sugar, maple syrup, salt and Prague powder #1 in a large pot over medium heat and stir until everything is dissolved. Cool it down fully in the refrigerator.

Lay the brisket out and trim off all the fat. Slice the brisket into two 4-pound (1800-g) pieces. This makes it more manageable moving forward. Place each piece in a separate bag. Fill each with half the brine mixture and seal it up, making sure you take out as much air as possible from each one. Now place each bag inside another bag. That way, if it leaks, it won't end up all over your fridge. I speak from experience here.

Lay them flat on the bottom shelf of the fridge and flip them once a day for 8 days. We shall return!

Joe Gatto's
from scratch

JUST DILL IT SPICY PICKLES

I adore from-scratch pickles. They are easy, delicious and super fun. I love how you can adjust the flavors however you like—sweet, spicy, garlicky, whatever your heart desires. Mine are spicy, smoky and really tangy. Perfect for a sandwich, making relish or just snacking out of the jar. Try pickling other veggies as well, such as onions, peppers, even cauliflower! Use different vinegars. Whatever you like, go crazy! I use these for my amazing pickle relish as well.

PREP TIME: 30 MINUTES

PICKLING TIME: 24 HOURS MINIMUM

MAKE THESE 3 DAYS BEFORE CREATING THE REUBEN

YIELD: THREE 1-PINT (475-ML) JARS

2 lb (900 g) fresh pickling cucumbers

6 cloves garlic, smashed

4 serrano peppers, cut in half

1 yellow onion, cut into quarters

2 red peppers, cored, seeded and sliced into 2-inch (5-cm) strips

1 sprig fresh dill

2 tsp (2 g) red pepper flakes

2 tsp (3 g) peppercorns

1 cup (240 ml) apple cider vinegar

1 cup (240 ml) white vinegar

2 cups (475 ml) water

2 tsp (10 g) sugar

2 tbsp (36 g) kosher salt

3 (1-pint [475-ml]) clean mason jars

First things first: wash and dry the cucumbers. Then slice them into spears and remove the blossom end. Why? The blossom end contains an enzyme that makes the pickles soft, and who wants a soft pickle? Nobody! Be sure to try to keep them all the same size. If they're not perfect, don't panic: they are still going to rock—they're a From Scratch pickle!

(continued)

JUST DILL IT SPICY PICKLES (CONTINUED)

Next, evenly divide the garlic, serranos, onion, red peppers, fresh dill, red pepper flakes and peppercorns between the jars. Pack the cucumber slices into the jars. Trim the spears a little if they're too tall. Pack them in tightly but don't crush them together.

Combine the vinegars, water, sugar and salt in a Dutch oven. Bring it all to a boil for 2 minutes. Make sure everything is dissolved. Then carefully pour the brine over the pickles, filling until ¼ inch (6 mm) from the top.

Tap the jars to get rid of air bubbles and let the pickles settle. CAREFUL! The jars are going to be lava HOT! After tapping them, if there is a little more room, add a touch more of the brine.

Put the lids on tight and let your pickles cool down. Then refrigerate. I know it's tempting, but let them sit in the fridge for at least 24 hours. It's worth it. They will keep for up to a month, but trust me—they won't last that long.

INFUSED BUTTER

Making your own butter? Has Joe lost his mind? It's possible, but it's not over making butter! Delectable on toast, bagels and fresh pasta, this butter would make a chef's shoe taste like filet mignon. Change the flavors up however you like—red pepper flakes, sage, anything you want. Just do it!

PREP TIME: 1 HOUR 15 MINUTES

INACTIVE COOK TIME: 24 HOURS

WHIPPING TIME: 15 MINUTES

MAKE THIS 2 DAYS BEFORE CREATING THE REUBEN

YIELD: 1 CUP (225 G)

2 cups (480 ml) heavy cream
2 sprigs rosemary
6 cloves garlic, smashed
1 tsp (6 g) kosher salt

Place the cream in a small pot; add the rosemary sprigs, smashed garlic cloves and salt. Place over medium heat and bring to a simmer. Simmer for 5 minutes, stirring occasionally. Take off the heat and let it steep for 1 hour.

Place in a glass bowl and put in the fridge overnight. Strain the solids out and place into the bowl of a stand mixer. Turn it on medium with the whip attachment. After about 5 minutes, you will see the cream begin to thicken. Keep beating until it's whipped cream. Grab a towel here, it's going to start splattering soon. The whipped cream will now begin breaking down into butter and buttermilk.

Once the butter and buttermilk separate, about another minute, stop the mixer and strain. Save the buttermilk for another use like biscuits or bread. Fill a bowl with ice-cold water and wash your butter. This helps keep your awesome butter from spoiling too quickly. Now hurry up and spread this on your homemade rye bread and make your Reuben!

RYE BREAD

Making your own bread is so satisfying and it's super delicious. Plus, you can change the flavors to make it just right. It takes some time, but when you make the Reuben with this ... LOOK OUT! Once it's cooled, be sure to wrap tightly in plastic wrap so it will stay fresh for the Reuben the next day. If you must, slice a piece and eat it. Be warned, though, one leads to two and two leads to three ...

PREP TIME: 20 MINUTES

RISE TIME: 2 HOURS AND 15 MINUTES

COOK TIME: 45 MINUTES

MAKE THIS THE DAY BEFORE YOU CREATE THE REUBEN OR PASTRAMI SANDWICH

YIELD: 1 LOAF

1 cup (240 ml) warm whole milk, warmed to 110°F (43°C)

1 tbsp (15 ml) molasses

1 tbsp (15 ml) honey

2¼ tsp (9 g) active dry yeast

1¼ cups (150 g) rye flour

2¼ cups (270 g) all-purpose flour, plus more for dusting

2 tsp (12 g) kosher salt

1½ tbsp (11 g) plus ¼ tsp caraway seeds, divided

4 tbsp (60 g) Infused Butter (page 49), melted

1 egg

1 tsp (3 g) cornmeal, plus more for dusting the pan

Egg wash made of 1 large egg beaten with 1 tbsp (15 ml) water

Combine the warmed milk, molasses, honey and yeast in a bowl and let it bloom for 10 minutes. In the bowl of an electric mixer, combine the rye flour and all-purpose flour. Finely grind the salt and 1½ tablespoons (11 g) of the caraway seeds together and add to the flour, whisking them together well.

Add the melted butter and egg to the bloomed yeast mixture, then add to the flour and beat at medium speed until the mixture forms a sticky ball, 2–3 minutes.

Remove the dough from the bowl. Place on a lightly floured surface and knead for 1 minute; it will become smooth. Using your hands, form the dough into a ball and place in a lightly oiled bowl. Cover with plastic wrap and set aside in a warm place until it doubles in size, about 1 hour and 15 minutes. I like to set it on the side of the oven as it preheats.

Remove the dough from the bowl, gently knead the dough 2 or 3 times and shape it into a log to fit the prepared baking pan. Again we are going to cover with some plastic wrap and set aside by the oven once more until it doubles in size, about 1 hour.

(continued)

RYE BREAD (CONTINUED)

Preheat the oven to 350°F (180°C, or gas mark 4) and lightly grease an 8½ x 4½-inch (21.3 x 11.7-cm) baking pan, sprinkle with some cornmeal and tap it to completely cover the sides.

Once the dough has risen, remove the plastic wrap. Using a pastry brush, brush the egg wash lightly over the top of the dough. Finely grind the remaining ¼ teaspoon caraway seeds and mix with the cornmeal; sprinkle the mixture over the top. Bake until brown, about 45 minutes, but it's best to use an internal thermometer. You are looking for an internal temperature of 190°F (88°C). Remove from the oven and cool on a rack. Now make your Reuben and love life!

RIDICULOUS RUSSIAN DRESSING

When you're making the Reuben you have to make the Russian dressing from scratch. This shows you're bringing your A game. Be sure to grate the horseradish yourself. It really makes the flavors pop! This also rocks with wraps and burgers and as a dip for our homemade Parmesan Herb Fries (page 34). You already made the ketchup and mayonnaise, so there's not much work left.

PREP TIME: 10 MINUTES

INACTIVE COOK TIME: 12 HOURS

MAKE THIS 1 DAY BEFORE CREATING THE REUBEN

YIELD: 1¾ CUPS (350 G)

3 tbsp (45 g) freshly grated horseradish, or to taste

2 tbsp (20 g) grated yellow onion

1 cup (190 g) Mayo That Rocks (page 26)

½ cup (95 g) Killer Ketchup (page 22)

Combine all the ingredients in a large bowl. Stir really well. You can use it right away, but I love to let it sit in the fridge overnight so the flavors really mingle and party together!

COOKING THE CORNED BEEF

PREP TIME: 30 MINUTES

COOK TIME: 8–10 HOURS

DO THIS THE DAY YOU ARE CREATING THE REUBEN

1 large onion, cut into 6 wedges

2 stalks celery, chopped

3 russet potatoes, halved

3 carrots, halved

1 recipe Kick-Ass Corned Beef (page 44)

12 oz (350 ml) dark beer

1 bay leaf

3 cloves garlic, smashed

1 head cabbage, cored and cut into 6 wedges

Lay the onion wedges, celery, potatoes and carrots in the bottom of a slow cooker. Place the corned beef on top and add the beer, bay leaf and garlic. Cook on low for 6 hours. Add the cabbage and cook for another 2–4 hours. Check it for tenderness at 8 hours. Take it out when it's ready to go. Let it cool for ½ hour and slice against the grain. Now you can make sandwiches or have a traditional corned beef dinner. Or you could make one of my favorites—corned beef hash with two over-easy eggs!

THE CORNED BEEF REUBEN

Make these for a Pats game and your friends will cheer for you like a Brady-to-Gronk touchdown!

PREP TIME: 15 MINUTES

COOK TIME: 10 MINUTES

IF YOU ARE MAKING THIS RIGHT NOW I AM SO JEALOUS OF YOU

YIELD: 4 SANDWICHES

4 tbsp (60 g) Infused Butter (page 49)

8 slices Rye Bread (page 51)

½ cup (120 ml) Ridiculous Russian Dressing (page 54)

8 slices Swiss cheese

2 lb (900 g) Kiss-Ass Corned Beef (page 44)

1 cup (150 g) Sauerkraut (page 41)

Just Dill It Spicy Pickles (page 47), for serving

Butter one side of each slice of rye bread. Spread the nonbuttered sides with the Russian dressing. Layer on 1 slice of Swiss cheese, a pile of ½ pound (230 g) corned beef, ¼ cup (38 g) of sauerkraut and another slice of Swiss. Place the other slice of rye, buttered side out, on top and griddle them up, 3–4 minutes a side. They should be golden brown. I like to finish them in a 350°F (180°C, or gas mark 4) oven for 5 minutes on a baking sheet to get the cheese super melty. Serve with the spicy pickles. YUM!

A SOULFUL PASTRAMI SANDWICH

I grew up eating these, getting the pastrami from a local deli. I remember watching the Red Sox game, eating one of these juicy, spicy creations topped with spicy mustard on my mom's homemade rye bread. Love it!

PERFECT PASTRAMI

We have conquered the corned beef! So now let's move on to the smoky, sexy pastrami. It's going to be the same curing process as the corned beef and then instead of just steaming, we rub, smoke and steam. See, that's not so hard, right? Plus, this is stupid yummy! Now this is the same cure as for the corned beef, but we don't trim all the fat because the fat is good on pastrami. The long smoke makes it melt in your mouth.

PREP TIME: 45 MINUTES

CURE TIME: 9 DAYS

MAKE THIS 9 DAYS BEFORE CREATING THE PASTRAMI SANDWICH

YIELD: 8–10 SERVINGS

1 gallon (3.8 L) water

¼ cup (47 g) Pickling Spice (page 43)

½ cup (90 g) brown sugar

¼ cup (60 ml) maple syrup

1 cup (288 g) kosher salt

2 tsp (10 g) Prague powder #1

8-lb (3600-g) beef brisket

4 (2-gallon [8-L]) zip-top bags

Place the water, pickling spice, brown sugar, maple syrup, kosher salt and Prague powder #1 in a large pot over medium heat and stir until everything is dissolved. Cool it down fully in the refrigerator.

Lay the brisket out and trim some of the fat, not too much because we are making pastrami, so the fat will melt and become yummy. Cut the 8-pound (3600-g) brisket into two 4-pound (1800-g) pieces. This makes it more manageable moving forward.

Place each 4-pound (1800-g) piece in a separate bag. Fill each with half the brine mixture and seal it up, making sure you take out as much air as possible from each one. Now place each bag inside another bag. That way, if it leaks it won't end up all over your fridge. I speak from experience here. Lay them flat on the bottom shelf of the fridge and flip them once a day for 8 days.

PASTRAMI RUB

The rub is an important part of the kick-butt pastrami. This has a little kick from the red pepper flakes. Yum. This works great on chicken as well!

COOK TIME: 15 MINUTES

MAKE THIS 1 DAY BEFORE CREATING THE PASTRAMI SANDWICH

YIELD: ABOUT ¾ CUP (88 G)

5 tbsp (25 g) whole peppercorns
3 tbsp (15 g) coriander seeds
1 tbsp (4 g) red pepper flakes
1 tbsp (12 g) palm sugar
1 tbsp (11 g) brown mustard seeds
1 tbsp (11 g) yellow mustard seed
1 tsp (4 g) smoked paprika
2 tsp (6 g) roasted garlic powder

In a spice grinder, pulse the peppercorns 3 times to get a course grind. Pour them into a bowl. Then pulse the coriander 2 times and add to the bowl. Add the rest of the ingredients and stir to combine. Store in a sealed container.

SALT 'N' VINEGAR CHIPS WITH A KICK!

Who doesn't love a salt 'n' vinegar chip with a sandwich? If you don't, I just don't think we can be friends. Sorry. These chips have some intensity from jalapeño powder. Addicting is an understatement. After you make these you might need to get a loved one to hold an intervention. Do these as your pastrami rests. That way they will be nice and crunchy!

PREP TIME: 45 MINUTES

COOK TIME: 15 MINUTES

MAKE THESE 1 HOUR BEFORE CREATING YOUR PASTRAMI SANDWICH

YIELD: 4 SERVINGS

1 lb (450 g) russet potatoes

1 cup (240 ml) white distilled vinegar

2 tbsp (16 g) vinegar powder

1 tsp (4 g) jalapeño powder

2 tsp (12 g) salt

1 qt (950 ml) canola oil

Wash the potatoes and slice ⅛ inch (3 mm) thin or use a mandoline if you feel more comfortable. Place the potatoes in a large bowl of cold water (they should be completely covered) and let them soak for 30 minutes. Change the water and add the vinegar. Let them soak for 30 minutes more. This removes the excess starch and will help them to be crisp!

In a spice grinder, add the vinegar powder, jalapeño powder and salt and take it for a spin for a minute. I like the uniformity of the mixture by doing this. Pour it into a small bowl and set aside. Take the chips out of the soak and dry them completely! They will splatter like crazy if you don't do this.

In a large Dutch oven, heat the oil to 350°F (180°C). Working in small batches, carefully drop the potatoes in and fry them up. They take about 5 minutes. Be sure to move them and flip them. Using a spider or slotted spoon, take the chips out and let them drain on paper towels. While they are still warm, hit them up with the spice mix, tossing them all around in it.

SMOKING AND STEAMING THE PASTRAMI

PREP TIME: 20 MINUTES

SMOKE TIME: 2–4 HOURS

STEAM TIME: 2–2½ HOURS

REST TIME: 1 HOUR

DO THIS THE DAY YOU ARE CREATING YOUR PASTRAMI SANDWICH

1 recipe Perfect Pastrami (page 60)

Canola oil

1 recipe Pastrami Rub (page 62)

Applewood and hickory chunks

When the 8 days are up, remove the briskets from the brine and rinse them well. Place them on a baking sheet and pat them dry with paper towels. Now spread a little canola oil on them and cover them with your pastrami rub.

Place them in the fridge while you set up the smoker. Get your smoker up to between 225°F and 250°F (105°C and 120°C). I use a combination of applewood and hickory. Stick your internal thermometers in horizontally and place your briskets, fat-side up, in the smoker. We want to bring the briskets up to 160°F (71°C); this could take up to 4 hours.

Now when they're done smoking, I like the traditional method of steaming them to make them super tender. I use my tamale steamer for this. Fill the steamer with water and bring it to a boil, then turn down the heat to medium. Place the internal thermometers in the pastramis again and carefully place them in the steamer. Reminder: the steam is hot, so watch out! Place the lid on and slowly steam them to 200°F (93°C), 2–2½ hours. Sometimes it takes a little longer than this; don't panic, just keep steaming them until they get tender. Remove them and let them rest for an hour. Then slice AGAINST the grain and eat a piece because you know you want to and then start building a sandwich!

A SOULFUL PASTRAMI SANDWICH

Another sandwich that just hits the spot when done right.

PREP TIME: 5 MINUTES

SATISFACTION TIME: ETERNITY

YIELD: 4 SANDWICHES

4 tbsp (44 g) Fiery and Zesty Mustard (page 25)

8 slices Rye Bread (page 51)

2 lb (900 g) Perfect Pastrami (page 60)

Salt 'n' Vinegar Chips with a Kick! (page 63), for serving

Slather some mustard on each slice of bread and pile on the pastrami. Then place another piece of rye on top, grab some chips and have at it!

Chef Joe Gatto

PASTA: THE ELIXIR OF LIFE

Who can resist a heaping bowl of steaming fresh pasta, smothered in a tangy, rich marinara and topped with freshly grated Parmesan? Of course you need a side of crunchy garlic bread fresh out of the oven to mop up all that extra sauce, right? I remember those smells wafting into my bedroom when I was a kid—the garlic, onions and tomatoes. Mom was making sauce and I would sprint down the stairs to help. Which really means taste! My stomach just growled like a caged tiger.

Fresh pasta is astonishing. It can cure a skinned knee, make an abysmal day blissful and even be a powerful aphrodisiac. It's true. Okay, let me explain. Back in the day, I was directing an independent feature film called *Overserved*. We needed an assistant director on the set and my good friend and cinematographer Tony Flanagan suggested a young lady he had worked with on his last project. A meeting was set and I met my wife-to-be, Carey Zolper, over coffee. We instantly hit it off—she is beautiful, tenacious and a bit of a troublemaker. My kind of woman. We started dating and I couldn't wait to cook for her. When I did, I pulled out the big guns: fresh pasta and from-scratch marinara. After polishing off the bowl she dubbed it the greatest pasta ever and christened my marinara "Liquid Gold." Fast-forward twelve years and we are still in love, have two wonderful kids and now we make the pasta all together. Ya gotta love pasta.

I make all kinds of pasta, from roasted butternut squash ravioli to hand-formed tortellini. There is something Zen about it. It's fun. I like fun. You can make it with your family, invite friends over to join you and have a blast; plus, when you tell them that they are going home with homemade pasta they will bring booze. Yes! At the end you get an incredible meal and a memory that will last forever.

We have determined that pasta is pretty kick-butt. Delectable, entertaining and gets you free booze. You know what else it is? Easy to make. Seriously, it's so easy. By hand or in a food processor, it doesn't matter. In this chapter I'm going to show you how. Imagine the next party when you break out handmade tortellini stuffed with three cheeses and topped with a roasted pistachio pesto! Stuff legends are made of. Let's get cranking and turn your kitchen into one straight from Italy.

PERFECT PASTA

Easy and fun from-scratch pasta is a soul-satisfying meal. This pasta recipe is simple, made with ingredients you will definitely have at home.

PREP TIME: 10 MINUTES

REST TIME: 30 MINUTES

MAKE THIS THE DAY YOU ARE CREATING FETTUCCINI CARBONARA, TORTELLINI OR RAVIOLI

YIELD: 1 POUND (455 G)

2 cups (240 g) all-purpose flour (unpacked), plus more for dusting

3 eggs

1 tsp (6 g) salt

Add the flour to a food processor along with the eggs and salt. Take it for a whirl. It will begin to look like coarse sand and then it will collect into a ball and clean up the sides of the food processor. If it doesn't come together right away, drizzle in water, a teaspoon (5 ml) at a time, until it does. Don't add too much water or the dough will get sticky.

Transfer the dough to a lightly floured countertop and knead for 5 minutes, or until the pasta springs back to the touch. Wrap it in plastic and store in the fridge for 30 minutes. Then you will be ready to start rolling the pasta of your choice!

dd flour to your processor.

Add eggs to the flour and process.

it's too dry, add water in very small increments.

Pasta dough! You did it!

FETTUCCINI CARBONARA (THIS RECIPE IS *NSYNC!)

I showed Joey Fatone from *NSYNC how to make this on his show, *My Family Recipe Rocks*. Joey and his crew flipped out at how ridiculously tasty it was. I mean, flipped out!

FANTASTIC FETTUCCINI

Fettuccini at home! With our homemade pasta dough already in the fridge, this is a snap. You can have it made fresh before someone could go to the store and buy pasta, and this is otherworldly. This is a great one to do with the kids. They love to crank and see the beautiful strands of pasta flowing from the pasta machine.

PREP TIME: 20 MINUTES

COOK TIME: 3–4 MINUTES

MAKE THIS THE DAY OF OR DAY BEFORE THE FETTUCCINI CARBONARA

YIELD: 1 POUND (455 G)

1 recipe Perfect Pasta (page 71)

Remove the dough from the fridge. Make sure you have your pasta roller ready to go, secured down on a countertop. Divide the dough into 4 equal pieces. Take one and set it aside. Place plastic wrap over the others so they don't dry out. Take the piece of dough and make a ½-inch (1.3-cm) thick disk. Roll it through the largest setting. Bring the ends of the dough toward the middle and press down to seal, like folding a letter into thirds; we are creating straight sides. Roll it through the 1 setting again. If the dough is at all sticky, lightly dust it with flour. Without folding again, begin to roll the pasta thinner by putting it through the machine repeatedly, narrowing the setting each time up until 5.

Place the cutting attachment onto the pasta roller. Take the pasta sheet and feed it through and boom! Fettuccini! Set the fettuccini aside, making sure none of it touches each other. If not, it will stick together and make a huge clump. Not cool. Or you can hang it on a pasta rack if you like.

When ready to cook, bring a large pot of heavily salted water to a boil over high heat. Place the pasta in and in 2–3 minutes you can drain and be ready to eat! Or set the dry pasta aside to make Fettuccini Carbonara (page 79).

FETTUCCINI CARBONARA

This is not a dish you want to eat every night, but when you do, look out! SOOOO GOOOD! The from-scratch bacon and pasta bring it to deity status.

PREP TIME: 20 MINUTES

COOK TIME: 15 MINUTES

YIELD: 4 SERVINGS

1 recipe Fantastic Fettuccini (page 76)

1 tbsp (15 ml) olive oil

8 oz (230 g) Maple Chipotle Bacon (page 17), cut into ½-inch (1.3-cm) cubes, or pancetta

2 tbsp (22 g) minced garlic

3 egg yolks

½ cup (120 ml) heavy cream

1 tsp (2 g) red pepper flakes

1 cup (100 g) freshly grated Parmesan

1 tbsp (15 ml) fresh lemon juice

Salt and pepper

2 tbsp (5 g) julienned fresh basil

First thing we need to do is cook our from-scratch pasta. Heavily salt a large pot of water and bring it to a boil over high heat. Toss in the fettuccini and cook for 3–4 minutes. Once it's nice and tender, take it out with a slotted spoon and put it in a bowl. Hold onto that pasta water.

Place your favorite large sauté pan over medium heat, add the olive oil, just to coat, and toss in the bacon cubes. Sauté until the bacon is browned and crispy. Toss in the garlic and sauté for about 30 seconds, moving it around constantly.

Now it's fettuccini time. Add the cooked and drained pasta to the pan and toss it around in the fat until it's coated. Beat the egg yolks, cream, red pepper flakes and Parmesan together really well. Now this part needs to happen quickly. Slide the pan off the heat and pour the egg and cheese mixture straight into the pasta, stirring constantly; you don't want pasta and scrambled eggs. We are looking for this to thicken. I know its crazy but the sauce will thicken. Stir in the lemon juice. Now to get it super creamy, add some of your pasta water, ½ cup (120 ml) at a time, until it's velvety. Season it up with salt and pepper, sprinkle on the fresh basil and stand back!

TERRIFIC THREE-CHEESE TORTELLINI WITH ROASTED TOMATO MARINARA

Tortellini, oh how I love thee. I love to teach people how to make these. Their faces light up as you turn a flat piece of pasta into a mouthwatering little piece of art filled with love. The ones below are going to be a huge hit, especially with the roasted marinara! Feel free to experiment with different fillings. The possibilities are endless. Don't forget, these are awesome in a soup as well! Your mind is racing with ideas, isn't it?

RICOTTA BRILLIANCE

Creamy, soft and a little sweet, this cheese can be used for both savory and sweet dishes. From lasagna and tortellini to cannoli and cheesecakes, this splendid cheese is as versatile as it is super simple to make. This ricotta is amazing on grilled bread with olive oil and sun-dried tomatoes, or mixed with the Toasted Pistachio Basil Pesto Sauce (page 95) it's perfect for stuffing tortellini. Or just add a little salt and pepper and eat it right out of the bowl! You can use the whey to feed your plants (they love it) or in breads and soups!

PREP TIME: 10 MINUTES

COOK TIME: 10 MINUTES

DRAIN TIME: 60 MINUTES

MAKE THIS THE DAY BEFORE YOU CREATE THE THREE-CHEESE TORTELLINI

YIELD: 3 CUPS (710 G)

3 cups (700 ml) whole milk
2 cups (475 ml) heavy cream
1½ tsp (9 g) kosher salt
2 tbsp (30 ml) lemon juice
1 tbsp (15 ml) white vinegar

In a 2-quart (1.8-L) saucepan over medium heat, combine the milk, cream and salt. Bring to a boil. Turn it down to a simmer and then add the lemon juice and vinegar. Stir it around to fully incorporate the acids. Simmer for 2 minutes while the curds separate from the whey. Take it off the heat and let it stand for 10 minutes.

While the ricotta sits, line a large colander with moistened cheesecloth and place it over a smaller bowl so curds don't sit in the whey. Pour the ricotta into the colander. Let it drain for 60 minutes. If you let it drain longer, the ricotta will get firmer, so experiment and see what you like. It will firm up considerably overnight, and even more the following day, so even if it doesn't seem as firm as you want it, there's no need to drain for more than an hour. Once it's done draining, it's ready to eat.

CAREY'S ROASTED TOMATO MARINARA

Just thinking of the incredible aromas the house fills with when I start making sauce brings me back to my childhood. I love to make extra and freeze it. There is nothing like having garden-fresh marinara in the middle of winter when it's bitter cold outside. It warms the body and the soul. This hooked my wife for life when I made it for her, so of course I named it after her!

PREP TIME: 20 MINUTES

COOK TIME: 2 HOURS 20 MINUTES

MAKE THIS THE DAY BEFORE CREATING THE THREE-CHEESE TORTELLINI

YIELD: 5 CUPS (1200 G)

1 head garlic

2 tbsp (30 ml) extra-virgin olive oil, divided

1 sprig rosemary, leaves chopped

20 sprigs thyme

15 sprigs oregano

5 lb (2250 g) whole fresh Roma tomatoes

1 medium yellow onion, quartered

1 tbsp (18 g) sea salt

1 tsp (3 g) fresh cracked pepper

1 tsp (2 g) red pepper flakes

1–2 cups (240–480 ml) Homemade Chicken Broth (page 174)

2 tbsp (30 ml) balsamic vinegar

1 tbsp (6 g) julienned fresh basil leaves

Preheat your oven to 350°F (180°C, or gas mark 4). Slice ¼ inch (6 mm) off the top of the head of garlic. Drizzle 1 teaspoon (5 ml) of the olive oil on it and wrap it tightly in foil. Set aside.

Line 2 baking sheets with foil and grease with olive oil. Spread out the rosemary, thyme and oregano on the baking sheet evenly. Slice all the tomatoes in half lengthwise and place in a bowl with the onion. Drizzle with the remaining 1 tablespoon and 2 teaspoons (25 ml) olive oil and sprinkle with the salt, black pepper and red pepper. Toss to coat and set aside. Lay the tomatoes and onion on the herbs cut-side up, along with the wrapped garlic head. Bake in the oven for 1½ hours. Remove the garlic bulb (use tongs) after 1 hour, open the foil and set aside to cool. Turn the oven to 400°F (200°C, or gas mark 6) and roast the tomatoes and onion for 20 more minutes, until they start to caramelize. When they are done, remove those bad boys from the oven and place in a large pot on the stove. Pour any remaining juices into the pot as well. Discard the herbs. Pop the garlic from their skins into the pot. Blend with a stick blender until smooth. If the sauce is a little thick, add the chicken broth ½ cup (120 ml) at a time. Add the balsamic vinegar and cook over low heat for 30 minutes. Stir in the basil, then taste and season with more salt and pepper. Yum. Let cool and store in the fridge.

oast the tomatoes and onions until carmelized.

Blend carefully.

et a smooth consistency.

Add some basil and chow down.

TERRIFIC THREE-CHEESE TORTELLINI WITH ROASTED TOMATO MARINARA

Tortellini are a blast to make by hand. Kids and adults love to do this at parties. So come on, let's get going!

PREP TIME: 30 MINUTES

COOK TIME: 3–4 MINUTES

YIELD: 4–6 SERVINGS

FILLING

1 cup (190 g) Ricotta Brilliance (page 82)

½ cup (95 g) shredded Fresh Mozzarella Is God (page 105)

¼ cup (22 g) freshly grated Parmesan

¼ cup (12 g) chopped fresh basil

1 egg, beaten

1 tsp (3 g) fresh cracked pepper

1 tsp (6 g) sea salt

1 recipe Perfect Pasta (page 71)

All-purpose flour, for dusting

1 recipe Carey's Roasted Tomato Marinara (page 85)

Freshly grated Parmesan, for serving

For the filling, place all the ingredients in a large bowl and mix until combined. Taste it. Be happy. Add more salt and pepper if you like.

Divide the pasta dough into 4 equal pieces. Take one and set it aside. Place plastic wrap over the others so they don't dry out. Take the piece of dough and make a ½-inch (1.3-cm) thick disk. Roll it through the largest setting of your pasta machine. Bring the ends of the dough toward the middle and press down to seal, like folding a letter into thirds; we are creating straight sides. Roll it through the 1 setting again. If the dough is at all sticky, lightly dust it with flour. Without folding again begin to roll the pasta thinner by putting it through the machine repeatedly, narrowing the setting each time up until 5.

Cut the sheet of pasta into 4-inch (10-cm) rounds with a biscuit cutter. No biscuit cutter? Just use a juice glass or a wine glass! Place a tablespoon (15 g) of the yummy cheese mixture into the center of each round.

Wet your finger with water and run it along the edge of the round. This helps create the seal. Fold over the round to create a half moon. Holding both ends with your fingers, push the center with your thumb and then bring the ends together to form the tortellini. Set aside on a well-floured counter and cover with a damp towel until they are all formed.

Grab your marinara out of the fridge and warm it up in a saucepan. Bring a large pot of salted water to a boil and add the tortellini in batches. Cook until they float to the surface, 3–4 minutes. Take them out with a slotted spoon and place them gently into a colander to drain. Place some tortellini in a bowl and spoon some roasted marinara over it, sprinkle with fresh Parmesan and go to town!

:ut circles into the dough.

Fill with a tablespoon (15 g) of filling.

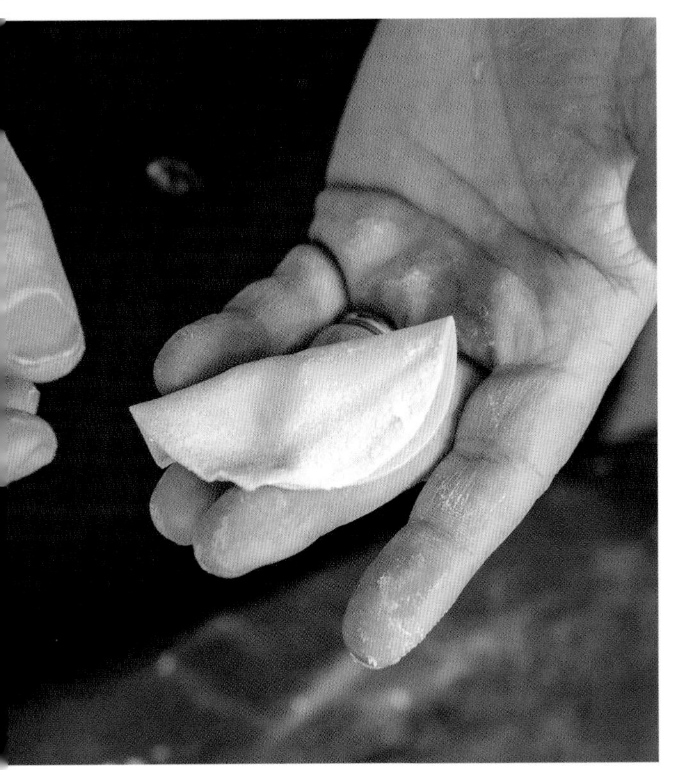

old in half.

Crimp the edges.

Push the center with your thumb.

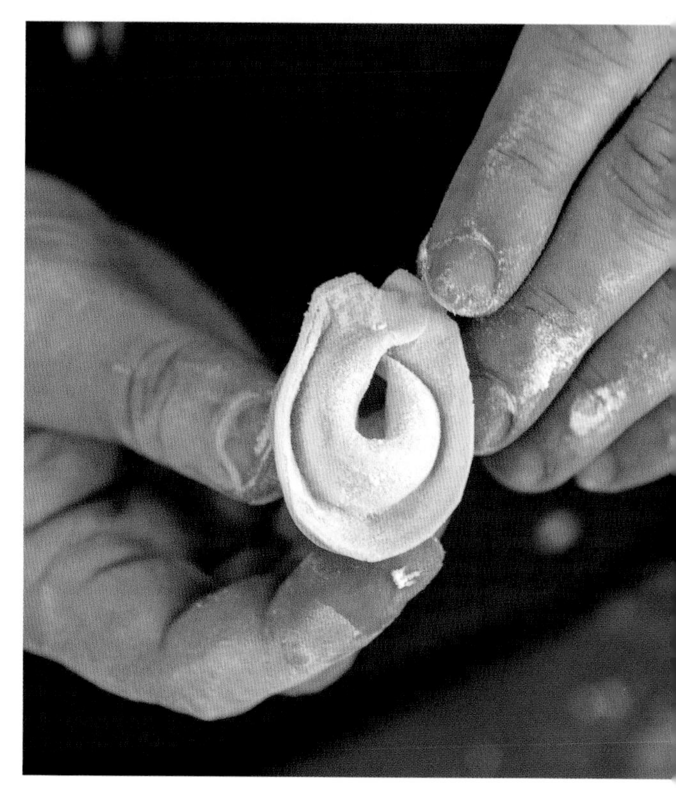

Bring the ends together.

You did it—awesome! From-scratch tortellini!

RAVENOUS ROASTED CHICKEN RAVIOLI WITH PESTO CREAM SAUCE

Ravioli is just one of those awesome things to make and eat. You can stuff it with anything. I call it a fridge cleaner. Extra chicken and ricotta? Stuff it in ravioli. Leftover roasted butternut squash? Hello, ravioli! Pulled pork? Rav it! Ground pork? Asian-style rav! Veggies going bad? Well, you get the idea. Anything is going to be remarkable. These chicken and pesto ravs are full of deep, rich flavors. The roasted chicken and creamy ricotta make an amazingly unctuous filling. Toss it with creamy pesto sauce and you have an instant best-friend maker. These are really fun to make with a lot of people, kids included. You supply the rav-making materials; your comrades supply the labor and booze. These freeze very well, so make a bunch and freeze them off in trays, then portion them out and have an amazing ready-made meal. Even frozen they cook in just a couple of minutes. Nice!

Pesto in the raw form.

Getting ready to become pesto.

Pistachio pesto! So yummy!

STEP 1 OF 2 FOR RAVENOUS ROASTED CHICKEN RAVIOLI WITH PESTO CREAM SAUCE

TOASTED PISTACHIO BASIL PESTO SAUCE

This is a great variation on the classic pesto made with pine nuts. Rich and deep in flavor, this goes with anything. I love to make a cream sauce with it and pour it over fresh pasta. Also amazing on grilled or baked chicken. The uses are endless! Go crazy and let me know what you come up with!

PESTO TIME: 20 MINUTES

COOK TIME: 10 MINUTES

MAKE THIS THE DAY BEFORE CREATING THE RAVIOLIS

YIELD: 2 CUPS (460 G)

½ cup (75 g) pistachios

4 cloves garlic

½ cup (45 g) freshly grated Parmesan

3 cups (120 g) fresh basil

½–1 cup (120–240 ml) olive oil

1 tbsp (15 ml) fresh squeezed lemon juice

1½ tsp (9 g) salt

1 tsp (3 g) fresh cracked pepper

1 cup (240 ml) heavy cream

Pour the pistachios into a dry pan over medium heat. Move the pan around until you see them just getting brown spots and you smell the pistachios wafting in the air. Do not walk away or text or tweet! They will burn quick! Grind the pistachios, garlic and Parmesan into a paste in a food processor, about 2 minutes. Add the basil and take it for a whirl, about 2 minutes. Taste. Add the olive oil in a steady steam until, well, it looks like pesto. Add the lemon juice and salt and pepper. Taste and adjust.

Place a sauce pot over medium heat and add the pesto and heavy cream. Stir until combined and simmer for 10 minutes, until thick and creamy, stirring constantly. Keep an eye on this because it will burn quick! Let cool and store in the fridge.

RAVENOUS ROASTED CHICKEN RAVIOLI IN TOASTED PISTACHIO BASIL PESTO SAUCE

Rolling pasta is very enjoyable to me. I enter an almost Zenlike state. Some pasta rollers have different settings, so it's tough to say which numbers to put it at; on my Atlas I roll it to a 5. Use yours and find the thickness you like best. My family and I like the 5, but maybe you will go a little thinner or thicker. That's the fun of making it from scratch; you get to decide on everything! You have the power!

PREP TIME 30 MINUTES

COOK TIME 3 TO 4 MINUTES

YIELD: 4–6 SERVINGS

2 cups (300 g) chopped roasted chicken

½ cup (75 g) Ricotta Brilliance (page 82)

¼ cup (22 g) freshly grated Parmesan

Salt and pepper to taste

1 recipe Perfect Pasta (page 71)

All-purpose flour, for rolling

1 recipe Toasted Pistachio Basil Pesto Sauce (page 95)

Olive oil

Grab a large bowl and mix the chicken, ricotta and Parmesan together. Give it a taste and add salt and pepper if you think it needs it. Taste it again. Why? Because it tastes awesome, that's why! Set it aside.

Divide the dough into 4 equal pieces. Take one and set it aside. Place plastic wrap over the others so they don't dry out. Take the piece of dough and make a ½-inch (1.3-cm) disk. Roll it through the largest setting. Bring the ends of the dough toward the middle and press down to seal, like folding a letter into thirds; we are creating straight sides. Roll it through the 1 setting again. If the dough is at all sticky, lightly dust it with flour. Without folding again, begin to roll the pasta thinner by putting it through the machine repeatedly, narrowing the setting each time up until 5.

Take the sheet and find the middle by folding it in half and lightly pressing a line. Don't let the pasta stick together when doing this. Slice into 2 equal pieces. On one sheet drop about 2 teaspoons (10 g) filling about 2 inches (5 cm) apart. When the sheet is full, dip your finger in water and run it between the filling piles on the pasta. Cover the filled sheet with the other sheet of dough.

Take your pesto sauce from the fridge and gently warm it up in a saucepan over medium-low heat. Keep an eye on it—it will burn easily. Once it's warm, turn off the heat and set aside.

(continued)

etting the filling down.

Putting the top on the ravs.

aking the ravs look pretty.

RAVENOUS ROASTED CHICKEN RAVIOLI IN TOASTED PISTACHIO BASIL PESTO SAUCE (CONTINUED)

Using your fingers, gently press on the top pasta sheet, working down to seal in the filling. Do not seal all the edges first; you don't want to trap air inside the ravioli. Once they are all pressed, use a knife or pizza cutter to cut the ravioli shapes. Crimp the edges with a fork and set aside. Bring a large pot of very salted water to a boil and add the ravioli. Cook for 3–4 minutes, or until they float. Using a large slotted spoon, grab them out of the water. Drain them well and place them into a bowl that has been brushed with olive oil. Toss them with the pesto sauce, grab a glass of wine and enjoy!

PIZZA IS A FOOD GROUP

It's true. Well, at least in my house it is. My family and I love pizza. My kids are insane for it and there is really something extraordinary about making it at home. Sliding it out of the hot oven and seeing the gooey mozzarella bubbling over the tangy red sauce in a mesmerizing dance is awe-inspiring. The crackling sound of the pizza cutter slicing through the crispy crust is music to my ears. Oh, and that first bite. Paradise.

I'm not kidding; this is what it's really like for me. The key is making it all from scratch. It's really easy and exciting. Making the dough is a snap; the sauce—it's a one-pot wonder. The mozzarella: once you make it there's no turning back. I'll show you how to take it even further if you want to take the plunge. How about making your very own charcuterie? That's right, your own pepperoni and salami. What? I know it's crazy, but you can do it!

Another fun thing about pizza is it's customizable. To each their own. Everyone in my family gets to construct his or her own personalized pie. Fun, yummy and very independent, which makes the kids super happy. Now, there is always a debate about what to cook pizza on at home. A pizza stone? Cast iron? Both great, but for me, I use the baking steel. What's the baking steel, you ask? Let me have my good friend Andris, creator of the baking steel, explain on page 114.

CHEESE PIZZA FROM HEAVEN

Just a plain cheese pizza? Easy does it—when you make it all from scratch it will blow you away! Now, of course you can pile on whatever you like: think of it as a blank canvas and you are the painter. Go, Picasso, go!

FROM-SCRATCH PIZZA SAUCE

If you're going to make pizza, you have to make the sauce. This is a must, people—no jarred sauce, please. The extra sauce goes perfect with pasta, mixed with rice or just for dipping fresh bread into. Mmmmmm ... dipping fresh bread. Now I'm starving! This stays great in the fridge for up to a week. Or freeze it for up to 6 months!

PREP TIME: 20 MINUTES

COOK TIME: 2 HOURS AND 20 MINUTES

MAKE 1 DAY BEFORE YOU MAKE YOUR PIZZA OR CALZONE

YIELD: 5 CUPS (1200 G)

1 recipe Carey's Roasted Tomato Marinara (page 85)
1 tsp (3 g) garlic powder
1 tsp (3 g) onion powder
¾ tsp dried basil
¾ tsp dried thyme
¾ tsp dried oregano
½ tsp ground fennel seed
¾ tsp sea salt
½ tsp fresh cracked pepper
½ tsp red pepper flakes

Combine the sauce with the seasonings, simmer over medium-low heat to blend the flavors and you're good to go!

FRESH MOZZARELLA IS GOD

For me, fresh mozzarella is God. Not the God but at least a demi-god. To eat it is at once wonderful, delectable and, for some, a religious experience. I know it is for me. When I'm nestled in my bed it's not sugarplums dancing in my head—it's gooey mozzarella. There is nothing like fresh mozz. Whether it's melted on a pizza hot out of the oven with all its love stretching the limits of space and time, or served chilled on a slice of fresh tomato with a few ribbons of basil scattered about, drizzled with olive oil and balsamic, it makes me swoon as if I were Scarlett O'Hara looking at Rhett. I learned this with my friend Sarah at New England Cheesemaking Supply Company. This is my take on their awesome recipe.

PREP TIME: 10 MINUTES

COOK TIME: 50–60 MINUTES

DRAINING TIME: 20 MINUTES

MAKE THIS THE DAY BEFORE YOU MAKE YOUR PIZZA OR CALZONE JUST UP TO THE FINISHED CURD STAGE! PULL IT FRESH THE DAY OF!

YIELD: 1 POUND (455 G)

- 1 gallon (3.8 L) whole milk
- 1½ tsp (8 g) citric acid dissolved in 1 cup (240 ml) water
- ¼ tsp liquid rennet added to ¼ cup (60 ml) water

Pour the milk into a large Dutch oven. Add the citric acid solution and gently stir it in. Heat the milk over medium heat, stirring constantly, to 90°F (32°C). Take the pot off the heat and add the rennet, stirring the whole time. Stir for 1 minute. Place the cover on the pot and leave it alone for 10 minutes and let it sit. Hey, I said let it sit! No peeking or touching!

Lift up the lid; your milk should have set and it should almost look like custard. Go ahead, gently poke it with your finger. It should spring back. Now take an offset spatula or bread knife (it has to be able to reach the bottom of the pot) and slice a grid pattern. This encourages the curd to release more whey. Put the Dutch oven back over medium heat and gently warm the curds in the whey to 105°F (40.6°C).

Place the curds into a strainer over a large bowl using a slotted spoon. Press down lightly on the curds to squeeze out more whey. Now let it sit for 20 minutes and let it drain even more.

Stop here if you are making the pizza the next day. The curd can stay in your fridge overnight. Pull it fresh the day of and you will have perfection!

(continued)

Curd!

Becoming mozz by constant heat. Almost there.

Let's stretch.

Whoa! Mozz!

from scratch
Chef Joe Gatto

Pulling the mozz.

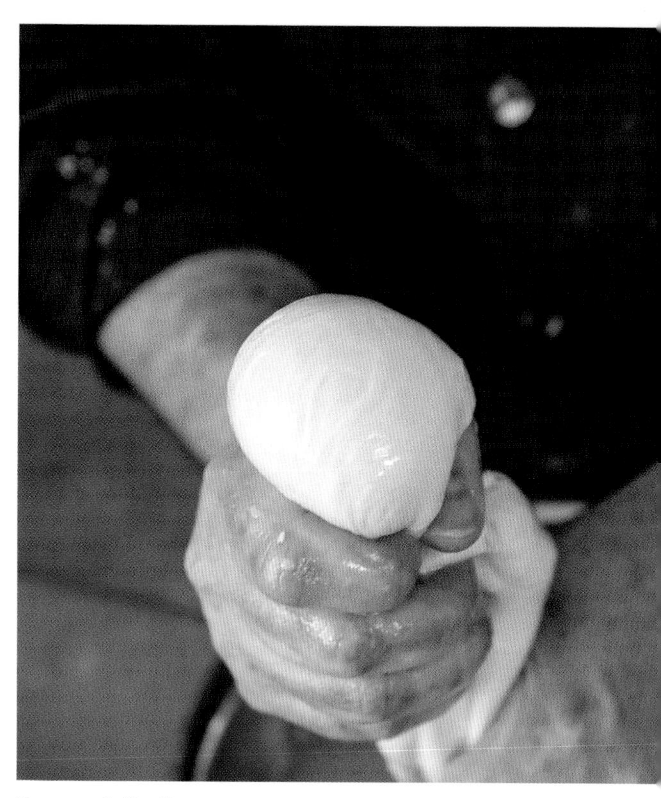

Squeeze it like it owes you money.

Mozz ball!

Keep going, Joe! They will all get eaten.

FRESH MOZZARELLA IS GOD (CONTINUED)

Now all you have to do is bring a pot of salted water to just below a boil, chop up the curd into 1-inch (2.5-cm) pieces and place in a large bowl. Gently pour the hot water over the curds. Just cover them by 1 inch (2.5 cm) or so. Let them sit to warm up for about 2 minutes. Start stirring the curds with a wooden spoon. You will see them begin to melt. Once they begin to melt, start lifting them and letting them stretch. Then place back in the bowl to warm up and stretch again. You are looking for a smooth, elastic and shiny appearance—almost like taffy. Drain and add new hot water. Repeat. Begin shaping into a ball, taking care not to overwork too much. Drop the ball into an ice-water bath to cool, and it will hold its shape. Stuff into pie hole immediately, do not pass go, do not collect $200. Store in water or oil and use for everything!

BEER PIZZA DOUGH/ REGULAR PIZZA DOUGH

I love pizza. I mean, I LOOOOVVVEE pizza! I have passed this gene on to my kids, big-time. That's why I created this dough, because when my kids want pizza, they want it now. Rising, punching down and waiting 24 hours is not in a five- or two-year-old's vernacular. So I needed fast dough that didn't take a whole day to rise. When you make it, it's ready to go! It's an instant pizza party! It's also great for calzones, pretzels and even cinnamon rolls!

PREP TIME: 20 MINUTES

MAKE THIS THE DAY OF CREATING YOUR PIZZA

YIELD: 1 POUND (455 G) DOUGH, ENOUGH FOR 2 PIZZAS

3¾ cups (420 g) all-purpose flour, plus more for dusting

½ tbsp (8 g) baking powder

½ tbsp (9 g) salt

12 oz (350 ml) good beer (use one you would drink; for Beer Pizza Dough), at room temperature, or warm water (for Regular Pizza Dough)

2¼ tsp (9 g) active dry yeast

1 tsp (4 g) sugar

1 tsp (5 ml) olive oil

In a large bowl, combine the flour, baking powder and salt; mix it really well. In a separate bowl, combine the beer, yeast and sugar; let sit until foamy, about 5 minutes, then add the olive oil. Combine the wet with the dry and stir. Just a heads-up: the dough will be sticky, really sticky. Don't worry, it's all good.

Dust your counter with flour. Dump the dough onto it and give it a light coating with the flour. Knead the dough for about a minute to make it pliable and smooth. Now take the dough and divide it into 2 equal parts to make 2 pizzas. You are now ready for pizza making! How exciting! You can use a rolling pin for this, which is easier, or use your hands if you want a challenge! The pizza keeps that light, airy quality when you use you hands. Feel free to place in the fridge for an hour or two or even overnight. It will rise a bit if you do that but it's all good. Just punch it down and make pizzas or calzones!

Yeast going in the pool.

The yeast starting to bloom.

Blooming!

Mix into dry ingredients.

FROM-SCRATCH SECRET
THE SCIENCE BEHIND THE BAKING STEEL

BY ANDRIS LAGSDIN, CREATOR OF THE BAKING STEEL

I first met Joe Gatto in 2013 on Twitter. Sounds strange, right? I must have retweeted one of his funny tweets or just thought to myself, "This guy is cool." (My first impression was spot-on: Joe is a star.) Anyway, we got to talking and he asked me the about the Baking Steel. So I told him my story and he wanted one. Next thing you know, we're slinging pizzas together at his studio in Lexington, Massachusetts, telling jokes and sipping cold beer. It doesn't get much better than that.

Joe's passion is relentless. It shows in everything he does. In the three or four years I've known Joe, he has gone from a personal chef to living his dream of creating his own television show, *From Scratch*. And this show is going to turn food shows upside down. Finally, a show we can all relate to; it's going to be big. In fact, by the time you are reading this, I bet it already is. Anyway, Joe and I have remained great friends since our first Twitter encounter.

One thing we have in common is a love of great pizza. In fact, you'd be hard-pressed to find anyone who doesn't crave a perfectly thin and beautifully crisp pizza crust. When it comes to defining a genuine Neapolitan-style pizza, the pizza must be cooked in a stone oven at around 900°F (482°C) for 60 to 90 seconds. It isn't just for definition's sake that a Neapolitan pizza needs to be cooked at an extremely high temperature for a short amount of time, though—it's actually very important for the finished product. That high temperature (resulting in such a quick cook time) gives the pizza that beautiful, crispy crust we all crave. But home ovens just can't get that hot—most max out at around 500°F to 550°F (260°C to 288°C). If you wanted your cook time to be just as fast, but you couldn't get the temperature as high as you need in your home oven, what could you do? The answer: Move heat as fast as you can by using a good conductor of heat. That's where the Baking Steel comes in.

THERMAL CONDUCTIVITY

As you could probably guess, the Baking Steel is made purely of steel, which has high thermal conductivity. That's just a fancy way of saying that heat moves very quickly from the steel's surface to whatever it's touching. Compared to ceramic (which is what the traditional pizza stone is made of), steel's thermal conductivity is eighteen times greater! Think of it this way: If you were to walk on ceramic bricks after they'd been sitting outside on a hot day, you wouldn't burn your feet. The heat transfer between the ceramic material and your feet would be pretty slow. (Slow enough that it wouldn't hurt, anyway.) However, if you tried doing the same thing with steel, you'd probably end up with some pretty severe burns—the heat would move much faster from the surface of the steel to your foot. (In other words, don't try this at home.) Basically, steel creates an environment that's hotter than it actually is, which is exactly what you need to create that perfect pizza crust!

THERMAL MASS

Steel isn't just a great conductor of heat—it also absorbs heat well. In scientific terms, the Baking Steel has a "high thermal mass." If you wanted to maintain a hot environment, one way to do it would be to heat up something heavy. That would ensure the area stayed hot even if its surrounding temperature became inconsistent. You can probably guess how this concept applies to the Baking Steel. When you're cooking pizzas one after another, the heat environment changes as you open and close the oven door. This affects the temperature of your oven, which in turn affects the cook time of your pizza. The Baking Steel solves this problem because steel is extremely dense—it holds in its heat, which means you don't have to worry about fluctuating oven temperatures.

PURE FACTS

Aside from the fact that the Baking Steel is great with heat, there are some other practical advantages. Anything made of ceramic will eventually shatter or crack if it's used for long enough. Those traditional pizza stones definitely won't last. Even professional pizza ovens that have 6-inch (15-cm) thick ceramic walls suffer from cracks. (If even that ceramic can't stand the heat, a pizza stone at home definitely won't!) Pizza stones also have the risk of heat shock—if you were to splash cold water onto a hot ceramic stone, there's a really good chance that it would shatter immediately. Baking Steel, on the other hand, is going to last. It's extremely durable (you'd have quite a time trying to break it), plus it has the added benefit of being impervious to any kind of heat shock. From a purely factual standpoint, it will last longer than any other at-home pizza-cooking tool.

CRAVING THAT SCIENTIFICALLY PROVEN CRUST?

When it comes to creating that perfect crust at home, the Baking Steel wins—no questions asked. After all, it was created with some precise scientific specifications in mind. (And you can't argue with facts!) But enough about science ... we know after reading all this, you're probably just ready for some of that mouthwatering pizza. So, go create some love on the Steel!

CHEESE PIZZA FROM HEAVEN

I always make two pizzas at my house because one of these would never be enough: my kids devour it. I love to use the Baking Steel (see page 114) to cook my pizzas on. If you don't have one you should get one. The pizzas and calzones come out perfect. Crispy, chewy, light and airy. A pizza stone will work, though not as well, as a substitute.

PREP TIME: 20 MINUTES

COOK TIME: 8 MINUTES PER PIZZA

YIELD: 2 PIZZAS

Flour, for dusting

1 recipe Beer Pizza Dough or Regular Pizza Dough (page 111)

Cornmeal, for dusting

1 cup (240 ml) From-Scratch Pizza Sauce (page 104)

16 oz Fresh Mozzarella Is God (page 105)

2 tbsp (10 g) freshly grated Parmesan

Place the baking steel or pizza stone in the oven and crank it to 500°F (250°C, or gas mark 10). A really hot oven equals a crispy crust.

Dust your counter with flour. Dump the dough onto it and give it a light coating of flour. Knead the dough for about a minute to make it pliable and smooth. Now take the dough and divide it into 2 equal parts. You are now ready for pizza making! How exciting! I do not like to use a rolling pin for this. Use your hands—it's fun! The pizza keeps that light airy quality when you use you hands.

Start in the center; use your fingers to press the dough to about ½ inch (1.3 cm) thick. Turning and stretching the dough as you go, make your pizza about 12 inches (30.5 cm) around. Pinch the edges to form the crust. Dust your pizza peel with cornmeal and place the dough on it.

Add half the sauce (reserving the rest for the next pizza) in an even layer and then dot it with half of the fresh mozzarella by tearing uneven-sized chunks and dropping them on. Sprinkle half the Parmesan all over the pizza. Launch onto your pizza stone or baking steel, cook for 4 minutes, give it a 180-degree turn and cook it for another 4 minutes, until the bottom is crispy. Keep an eye on it. Some ovens run hot and you don't want to burn it. While the first pizza is cooking, repeat to make a second pizza with the remaining ingredients. Remove the cooked pizza to a wire rack. Let it cool for a minute, slice it up and chow! Put the other pizza in the oven so it will be ready just when you are finishing the first one.

THE KING OF CALZONES. IT'S GOOD TO BE THE KING.

My mom always made calzones, and I worshipped them. Slicing into the crisp, airy crust and seeing the glistening spicy pepperoni as the gooey mozzarella oozed out ... mmmm! I couldn't get it into my pie hole fast enough! So when it was time to make my version, you know I was going all out. Make the charcuterie, the dough, the mozz—all of it. Tip to tail. I would describe how it felt when I took that first life-changing bite, but kids might read this book and it is not all age-appropriate.

PEPERONE! YOU MEAN PEPPERONI? NO. PEPERONE!

Nope, I spelled it correctly. This is the classic cured meat. It is very similar to pepperoni but is even deeper and richer. Now, curing you own meats is fun but also dangerous. You have to follow the steps exactly, and even then something might go wrong. If it doesn't smell good, don't eat it! No messing around. I adapted this recipe from my charcuterie guru, Dan Pagano.

PREP TIME, INCLUDING GRINDING AND STUFFING: 1½ HOURS

COOK TIME/FERMENTING: 6 WEEKS

MAKE THIS 6 WEEKS BEFORE THE CALZONE

YIELD: 4–6 LINKS

2 lb (900 g) top round

2 lb (900 g) hanger steak

1 lb (450 g) pork butt

¼ cup (144 g) kosher salt

1 tsp (6 g) pink salt #2 (nitrite)

1 tbsp (10 g) Bactoferm F-RM-52 (a live culture)

¼ cup (60 ml) distilled water

1 tbsp (9 g) cayenne

1 tsp (3 g) chipotle powder

1 tsp (3 g) smoked paprika

1 tsp (3 g) garlic powder

1 tsp (3 g) ground fennel seed

4 tbsp (60 ml) dextrose

2 tbsp (30 ml) dry red wine

6′ (2 m) hog casings, ½″ (1.3 cm) diameter, rinsed and soaked for an hour in clean water

Place your meat and grinding tools in the freezer for 1 hour. It makes it easier to trim and cube. Take it out; first things first, we are going to trim the beef, removing all the excess fat and sinew. Working quickly, slice both cuts of beef and the pork into 1-inch (2.5-cm) cubes. Now toss the cubes well with both salts. Grind into a large bowl using the ¼-inch (6-mm) die on the grinder. Set in the fridge.

Mix the Bactoferm F-RM-52 with the distilled water. Remove the grind from the fridge and then add the water mixture to the ground mixture. Add the cayenne, chipotle, paprika, garlic powder, fennel seed, dextrose and red wine and mix it all well in a mixer with a paddle attachment. Place back into the fridge for 1 hour while you set up the stuffer.

(continued)

PEPERONE! YOU MEAN PEPPERONI? NO. PEPERONE! (CONTINUED)

Stuff the peperone into the prepared hog casings, twisting the casings in one direction to tie off the length you want, and then twisting in the opposite direction for the next length of sausage. After you are done, place the sausages on a very clean surface, cover with clean kitchen towels and leave out at 75°F–85°F (24°C–30°C) for 12 hours to ferment.

Hang the sausage in a 50°F–60°F (10°C–15.6°C) environment with about 70 percent humidity and circulating air (at least a fan on them for an hour a day). If you don't have a basement for this, a converted wine cooler works really well. The peperone needs to hang out for approximately 6 weeks. They need to lose about 30 percent of their original weight. They need to be very firm to the touch. White mold is good to see. If it looks good and smells good, it should taste good!

9oz
8.5oz

THE KING OF CALZONES. IT'S GOOD TO BE THE KING.

These calzones are killer. Once you've tried my version, switch it up to include your favorite meats and cheeses.

PREP TIME: 20 MINUTES

COOK TIME: 15 MINUTES

YIELD: 4 KILLER CALZONES

1 recipe Beer Pizza Dough or Regular Pizza Dough (page 111)

All-purpose flour, for dusting

1 lb (450 g) Fresh Mozzarella Is God (page 105), cut into 1-inch (2.5-cm) slices

1 tbsp (3 g) chopped fresh basil

1 lb (450 g) Peperone (page 121)

Cornmeal, for dusting

1 recipe From-Scratch Pizza Sauce (page 104), for serving

Place the Baking Steel or pizza stone in the oven and crank it to 500°F (250°C, or gas mark 10). A really hot oven equals a crispy crust.

Divide the dough into 4 pieces. Take one piece and place the other 3 under a kitchen towel. Dust your counter with flour and begin to make a disk with the dough. Keep pressing and working outward until you have a 6- to 7-inch (15- to 18-cm) circle. On the half of the circle closest to you, place 2 ounces (56 g) mozzarella and sprinkle on some fresh basil. Be sure to leave a 1½-inch (3.8-cm) border so you can seal them after. Then layer on 4 ounces (113 g) peperone, 2 ounces (56 g) mozzarella and a sprinkle of fresh basil.

Now let's close the deal. Carefully fold the top half of the circle over the ingredients and seal the edges. If it's too dry, just dab a little water to help it seal. Once you've sealed it by hand, crimp the edges with a fork. Not only does this look cool but it also keeps everything from spilling out as the killer calzone cooks. Slice a couple of vent holes in the top of the calzone to let steam escape.

Repeat the process with the remaining 3 dough pieces; go ahead—I'll wait. Sprinkle cornmeal all over a pizza paddle. Gently place the calzones on and launch them onto the Baking Steel (see page 114) or pizza stone and cook for 12–15 minutes. Remove when brown and crispy. Place on a wire rack to cool. Serve with the pizza sauce for dipping.

VARIATIONS ON PIZZA: LAHMACUN AND TARTE FLAMBÉE

Over time I have been introduced to some cool variations on pizza. These are 2 of them! Give them a try if you are feeling cheeky!

Chef Joe Gatt

LAHMACUN

This is my take on the classic Turkish flatbread with lamb and tomatoes. It isn't the traditional one; I use my Beer Pizza Dough (page 111) and change around the components. This was inspired by one of the cameramen on my show. Multifaceted cameraman Adam Mikaelian is half-Armenian and he loved this pizza growing up, so I made my version for him and he devoured it like a zombie devours brains.

PREP TIME: 30 MINUTES

COOK TIME: 8–10 MINUTES

YIELD: 2 PIZZAS

FOR THE MEAT MIXTURE

¼ cup (65 g) tomato paste

2 tbsp (6 g) minced fresh parsley

1 tbsp (6 g) minced fresh cilantro

1 tbsp (3 g) minced fresh mint

4 cloves garlic, minced

1 jalapeño, minced (remove the seeds for less heat)

½ red pepper, seeded and diced

1 poblano pepper, seeded and diced

1 tsp (2 g) red pepper flakes

2 tsp (4 g) curry powder

1 tsp (2 g) ground cumin

1 tsp (2 g) smoked paprika

½ tsp allspice

6 oz (170 g) ground lamb

Cornmeal, for dusting

1 recipe Beer Pizza Dough or Regular Pizza Dough (page 111)

1 tbsp (15 g) Ricotta Brilliance (page 82)

2 plum tomatoes, diced small

½ cup (75 g) finely diced red onion

2 tbsp (6 g) minced fresh parsley

1 lemon

Place the Baking Steel or pizza stone in the oven and crank it to 500°F (250°C, or gas mark 10) for at least 30 minutes.

To make the meat mixture, combine the tomato paste and all the seasonings in a large mixing bowl and add the ground lamb. Mix everything together and set aside.

Sprinkle a pizza peel with cornmeal. Divide the dough in half. Roll both dough pieces into thin circles; we are looking for a ¼ inch (6 mm) thickness. Be sure not to roll your pizza out to a bigger size than your pizza peel, baking stone or Baking Steel, or bad things will occur. Transfer to the pizza peel. When you are finished, the dough round should have enough cornmeal under it to move easily when you shake the peel.

Spread half of the meat evenly over the disk of dough. Slide the flatbread onto the preheated steel. If you're using a sheet pan, place it right on the stone. Check for doneness in 5–8 minutes: the crust should be baked through but remain pale and soft. Remove to a baking rack or cutting board and repeat with next pizza.

Serve immediately with the ricotta, chopped tomatoes, onion, parsley and a squeeze of fresh lemon. Cut into slices or roll up the flatbread like a crepe and enjoy!

Lahmacun in raw form.

Chopping away.

Keep chopping, Joe!

Ground lamb.

ᴀdd the chopped ingredients.

Mix thoroughly.

ay out the dough.

Spread out topping evenly.

TARTE FLAMBÉE

Tarte flambée means "pie baked in flames." Awesome! When I was looking at different pizzas from around the world, this tasty French version was one that really stood out. It has bacon and caramelized onions: need I say more? This is my version of the classic.

PREP TIME: 40 MINUTES

COOK TIME: 60 MINUTES

YIELD: 2 PIZZAS

¾ lb (340 g) Maple Chipotle Bacon (page 17)

1 medium yellow onion, thinly sliced

1 medium red onion, thinly sliced

Pinch of kosher salt

1 recipe Beer Pizza Dough or Regular Pizza Dough (page 111)

Cornmeal, for dusting

1½ cups (360 g) Ricotta Brilliance (page 82)

2 tsp (3 g) red pepper flakes

2 tbsp (6 g) minced fresh parsley

2 scallions, thinly sliced, divided

Place the Baking Steel or pizza stone in the oven and crank it to 500°F (250°C, or gas mark 10). A really hot oven equals a crispy crust.

Grab your go-to cast-iron or sauté pan, place it over medium heat and cook the bacon until crispy. Drain on paper towels and crumble. Save 2 tablespoons (30 ml) of the fat for cooking the onions.

Place the onions into the hot pan with the reserved fat, sprinkle with some salt and begin sautéing over medium heat. Sauté for 20–25 minutes, moving the onions constantly and adjusting the heat to keep them from burning, until they are sticky, caramelized and yummy!

Divide your dough in half and roll both halves into a thin circle; we are looking for a ¼ inch (6 mm) thickness. Be sure not to roll your pizza out to a bigger size than your pizza peel, baking stone or Baking Steel, or bad things will occur. The tarte flambée is a thinner crust pizza. Poke a few holes in the top with a fork to prevent huge air bubbles. Dust your pizza paddle and transfer the dough to the peel. Carefully slide onto the Baking Steel or pizza stone. Cook each one for 5 minutes and rest on a cooling rack or cutting board when done.

(continued)

Dock the dough.

Mix the ricotta, red pepper flakes and parsley.

Spread it out.

Get those caramelized onions on there.

TARTE FLAMBÉE (CONTINUED)

While the crusts are baking, in a bowl, combine the ricotta, red pepper flakes and parsley. Divide between the crusts, spreading evenly. Then spread half your caramelized onions evenly over each pizza, then the bacon. Pop one of the pizzas onto your baking stone or Baking Steel and bake for 8 minutes, until the dough is crisp on the bottom and the toppings are lightly browned. Take it out of the oven and sprinkle with half of the scallions. Slice it up into triangles or squares and devour. Repeat with the second pizza. If there are leftovers, which I doubt, store in the fridge for a day or two.

from scratch
Chef Joe Gatto

RELEASE THE KRAKEN!

I'm a New England boy and seafood was everywhere when I was growing up. Except at my house. My idea of fresh fish growing up was fish sticks. Yeah, not a lot of seafood lovers at my house. As I got older and was more exposed to the food living in the nearby Atlantic, the more I appreciated it. The more I appreciated it, the more I began to marvel at locally caught fish and the flavors they had, tastes of the ocean and freshness.

But let's start at the beginning. When I was just a guppie my mom used to take me to Revere Beach, five miles (8 km) north of Boston. I loved it there; it was a little rough around the edges, but I remember it being so exciting. Gleaming cars cruising up and down the strip, throngs of people shimmering on the beach catching some rays, the cool, crisp sea air. But what I remember most was that I encountered my very first clam roll there.

It was just a shack of a place, but the smell permeated the strip and it was intoxicating. The lines were lengthy and the sun was scorching, but no one seemed to mind. Broad smiles materialized on people's faces as they received their rolls and rings, oil blotting through the brown paper bags. The anticipation was palpable. Finally, when it was our turn, my mom ordered. The hustle and bustle inside the tiny shack was incredible. The men moved at astronomical speed, efficiently banging out each order with precision. It was a fried food ballet.

The scruffy man barked out a number and my mom grabbed our food. I could see the onion rings peeking out from the top of the bag. I was so eager to dig in. We plopped on the nearby seawall. My mom handed me a slew of napkins and my bag. I dug right in. I'll never forget the crunchy fried clams as they melted in my mouth, tangy tartar sauce adding the perfect amount of zest, and oh, that soft bun. Incredible. The kicker was those onion rings—not battered loops of thick breading but crispy light strings of righteousness. I was hooked. The combination of the delicious food, the beach air and just chilling with my mom made for days I will never forget. Now, let's go make one from scratch!

FRIED CLAM ROLLS WITH ÜBER ONION RINGS

Crispy clams that melt in your mouth on a homemade hot dog bun with the tangy from-scratch Sriracha tartar sauce. This is the clam roll dreams are made of. I use the pretzel rolls for this and it's a treat beyond belief! Make the onion rings to go with these, shut off the phone, grab a comfy chair, sit down and enjoy.

Pulse

PERFECT PICKLE RELISH

This recipe redefines relish. I was never a huge relish fan; I always found it too sweet and one-note. By using our from-scratch pickles, we will make a condiment that punches that store-bought relish in the face. Zesty, spicy and full of flavor, this will blow your mind.

PREP TIME: 10 MINUTES

MAKE THIS 4 DAYS BEFORE THE CLAM ROLL

YIELD: 2 CUPS (480 G)

10 Just Dill It Spicy Pickles (page 47)

½ cup (80 g) pickled yellow onions (from Just Dill It Spicy Pickles)

2 pickled serranos (from Just Dill It Spicy Pickles)

2 pickled red peppers (from Just Dill It Spicy Pickles)

Place everything in a food processor and pulse 4–5 times. Store in the fridge for up to 4 weeks.

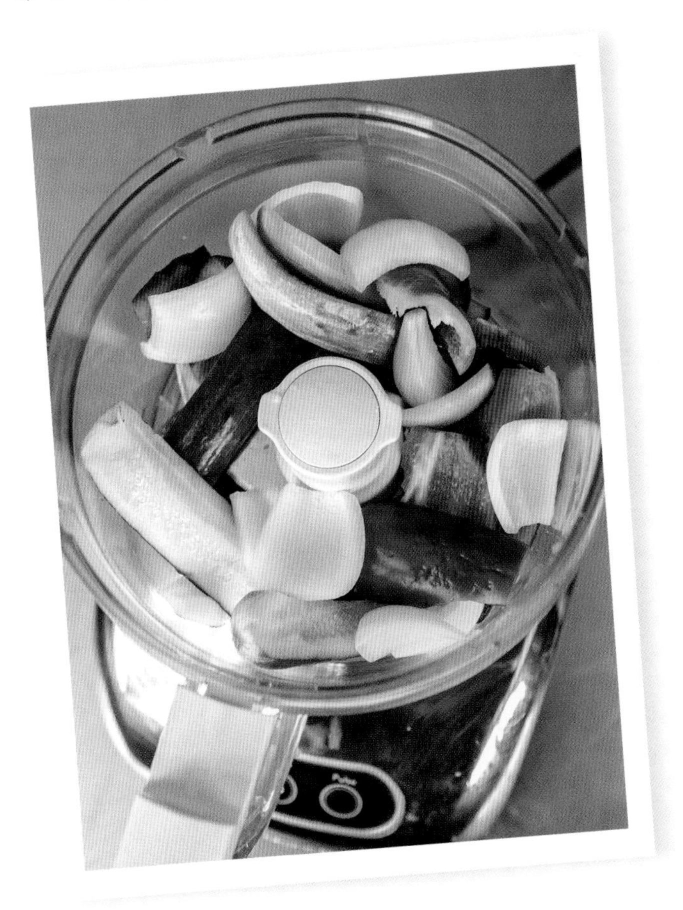

SIZZLING SRIRACHA

My go-to hot sauce. Spicy, rich and tangy. I literally just squirt this on homemade tortillas and eat them. It works so well to spice up any dish! I love the depth and complexity of this distinctive, fiery condiment.

PREP TIME: 10 MINUTES

COOK TIME: 15 MINUTES

MAKE THIS 2 DAYS BEFORE THE CLAM ROLLS

YIELD: 1½–2 CUPS (355–480 MML)

1 lb (450 g) red Fresno chiles

6 cloves garlic

2 tsp (12 g) kosher salt

3 tbsp (38 g) palm sugar

½ cup (120 ml) apple cider vinegar

½ tsp roasted red chili paste

¼ tsp fish sauce

¾ cup (180 ml) water

1 tbsp (15 (ml) fresh lime juice

First things first: remove the stems from the chiles and roughly chop them. Don't remove those seeds—we want that heat!

Combine the chopped chiles, garlic, salt, sugar, vinegar, chili paste, fish sauce and water in a pot over medium-high heat. Bring it all to a boil, then lower the heat and simmer for 10 minutes. After 10 minutes, remove from the stove and pour into a blender. Do not blend it right away; let it cool. It's dangerous to blend hot liquid.

When it's all cooled down, blend on the highest setting for 2–3 minutes, until it is very smooth. Place a strainer over a large bowl and pour the liquid in. Take a spatula and force the liquid through the strainer, leaving behind the solids. Remove the strainer and squeeze in the lime. Transfer it to a squeeze bottle and put it on everything from eggs to burgers! The longer it sits, the better it gets. It will last up to 2 months in the fridge but it will be long gone before then.

iracha in raw form.

Pepper getting ready to blend.

ending!

Force the liquid through the strainer.

SRIRACHA TARTAR SAUCE

This is a little twist on a typical tartar sauce. It has a nice touch of tang and heat from the sriracha. Awesome with any seafood, fried or not. But with the clam roll? Whoa.

PREP TIME: 10 MINUTES

MAKE THIS THE DAY BEFORE CREATING THE CLAM ROLLS

YIELD: 1½–2 CUPS (350–480 G)

1 cup (190 g) Mayo That Rocks (page 26)

2 tbsp (30 g) Perfect Pickle Relish (page 141)

1 tbsp (15 ml) Sizzling Sriracha (page 142)

1 tbsp (15 ml) fresh lime juice

1 tsp (3 g) fresh cracked pepper

Thoroughly combine all the ingredients in a glass bowl and set in the fridge overnight for the flavors to meld and party.

PRETZEL HOT DOG BUNS

When you're going to be making a clam roll from scratch, you can't just throw those gorgeous fried nuggets into any old bun. They need the star treatment, so let's give them it!

PREP TIME: 30 MINUTES

RISE TIME: 1 HOUR

COOK TIME: 12 MINUTES

MAKE THESE THE DAY OF THE CLAM ROLLS

YIELD: 6 LARGE BUNS

1½ cups (360 ml) whole milk, warmed to 110°F (43°C)

2 tbsp (24 g) packed dark brown sugar

2¼ tsp (9 g) active dry yeast

3¼ cups (390 g) all-purpose flour, divided, plus more for kneading

2 tbsp (28 g) Infused Butter (page 49), melted

1 tbsp (15 ml) olive oil

1 tsp (6 g) kosher salt

¼ cup (60 g) baking soda

4 cups (940 ml) warm water

3 tbsp (54 g) coarse salt

Combine the milk and sugar in a large bowl, stirring to dissolve the sugar, then sprinkle in the yeast. Let it bloom for 5 minutes. Pour it into a stand mixer with the dough hook, add 2¼ cups (270 g) of the flour and mix on low speed until moistened; increase to medium speed and run it for 2 minutes until a sticky dough is created. Add the melted butter, olive oil and kosher salt and run on low speed, and then add remaining 1 cup (120 g) flour; when it is moistened, increase the speed to medium and run for another 3 minutes, until the dough pulls away from the sides of the bowl. Place the dough onto a floured counter—it will be sticky—and knead it until smooth, adding more flour as necessary, a minute or two. Shape the dough into a ball, put it into a greased bowl, cover with a kitchen towel and put it in a warm spot to rise until it doubles in size, about 1 hour.

Preheat your oven to 450°F (230°C, or gas mark 8) and line 2 baking sheets with parchment paper. Turn the dough out onto a lightly floured surface and knead for 1 minute. Divide the dough into 6 pieces weighing approximately 5 ounces (140 g) each. Roll those pieces into 7-inch (18-cm) logs. Dissolve the baking soda in the warm water in a shallow baking dish or bowl. Dunk each log into the soda water and place onto the parchment-lined baking sheet. Cut a slit down the center about ½ inch (1.3 cm) deep. Sprinkle with the coarse salt and place them in the oven. Bake until golden, 10–12 minutes.

Pretzel buns in raw form.

Add wet ingredients to dry.

Mix away!

Kneading.

Shape into a log.

Getting hungry.

Don't slice too deep.

Kosher salt time.

ÜBER ONION RINGS

Onion rings are addicting, crunchy and salty, with just a touch of sweetness from the onion. MMMMM! These thin, crunchy loops of love are rehab-worthy, to be sure. I mean, you might walk into a room and all your friends will be sitting around to surprise you with an intervention! Love, love, love these!

PREP TIME: 15 MINUTES

MARINATING TIME: 1 HOUR

COOK TIME: 4–5 MINUTES PER BATCH

MAKE THESE RIGHT BEFORE YOU MAKE THE CLAM ROLLS

YIELD: 4 GENEROUS SERVINGS

1 cup (240 ml) buttermilk

2–4 tbsp (30–60 ml) Sizzling Sriracha (page 142)

1 tbsp (18 g) plus 1 tsp (6 g) kosher salt, divided, plus more for sprinkling

2 large yellow onions, peeled

1 cup (120 g) all-purpose flour

1 cup (160 g) masa harina

½ cup (80 g) cornmeal

2 tsp (10 g) baking powder

1 tbsp (9 g) chili powder

3 cups (700 ml) canola oil

In a large bowl, stir together the buttermilk, sriracha and 1 teaspoon (6 g) of the salt and set aside. Slice the onions into thin ¼-inch (6-mm) rings, separate them well, and place them into the buttermilk bowl. Place in the fridge for 1 hour. In a separate bowl, combine the flour, masa, cornmeal, baking powder, remaining 1 tablespoon (18 g) salt and chili powder.

Heat the canola oil in a large Dutch oven to 360°F (182°C). Place the dry ingredient mix into a shallow dish. In batches, take the rings out of the buttermilk and let the excess drain off for a moment, and then place into the dry mix. Toss them around to coat and gently place into the oil. Don't crowd the pot or the oil temperature will drop and they will get greasy. Let them fry for 4–5 minutes, until golden brown, gently moving and flipping to make sure they are all fried evenly. Remove them to paper towels to drain and sprinkle liberally with kosher salt.

FRIED CLAM ROLLS WITH ÜBER ONION RINGS

It's time to make these bad boys! I am so excited, I'm kind of freaking out! The clams need to soak for 3 hours, so be sure to take that into consideration. Use the same fry oil as you used for the onion rings if it's clean.

PREP TIME: 15 MINUTES

SOAKING TIME: 3 HOURS

COOK TIME: 1 MINUTE

YIELD: 6 SANDWICHES

2 cups (470 ml) buttermilk

2 tbsp (30 ml) Sizzling Sriracha (page 142)

2 tsp (12 g) salt, divided

1½ quarts (1344 g) fresh-shucked clams (I use littlenecks)

1 cup (120 g) all-purpose flour

½ cup (60 g) masa harina

½ cup (80 g) cornmeal

1 tsp (5 g) baking powder

1 tsp (3 g) garlic powder

1 tsp (3 g) onion powder

½ tsp smoked paprika

3 cups (700 ml) canola oil (see headnote)

1 recipe Pretzel Hot Dog Buns (page 147)

Sriracha Tartar Sauce (page 144), for serving

Über Onion Rings (page 151), for serving

Mix the buttermilk, sriracha and 1 teaspoon (6 g) of the salt in a large bowl and then add the clams. Cover and place in the fridge for 3 hours.

This is a great time to make the pretzel rolls!

In a large bowl, combine the flour, masa, cornmeal, baking powder, garlic powder, onion powder, paprika and remaining 1 teaspoon (6 g) salt. Pour it into a shallow baking dish for dredging. Place a colander in the sink and drain the clams. Heat the canola oil in a large Dutch oven to 360°F (182°C). Dredge the drained clams in the dry mixture until coated. Carefully drop the clams into the oil and fry for 60–90 seconds. They cook quickly, trust me; really keep an eye on them. They should be nice and golden.

Pull them out with a slotted spoon and place on a paper towel. Now they are ready to load into your amazing hot dog buns with your from-scratch tartar sauce. Try one now just to make sure they are awesome. Whoa! I said just one! Now load the rest into the buns and enjoy with the onion rings!

ww shucks.

Into the buttermilk bath.

oll in the flour mixture.

Eat these.

FROM-SCRATCH SECRET
AUTHENTIC CLAMBAKE

Everyone should do a clambake a least once, and once you do, you will want to do another one. The cool ocean breeze, the copious amounts of seafood slowly roasting under a blanket of seaweed, filling the air with the smells of New England, drinks in hand—good times are unavoidable. This really is an amazing way to spend time with your family and friends. We did one for the show this year and oh, man, what a blast! The kids were so into it, from swimming out to the rocks to source the seaweed to lighting a big ol' fire—they loved it from tip to tail. Not to mention the smorgasbord of delectable food and being able to chill on the beach all day. The clambake is really a straightforward thing—nothing fancy, just a little work and preplanning and you've got a killer party happening before you know it. Let's get started!

First thing you want to do is get a place locked down to have your clambake. Lighting a fire in the middle of a public beach will not go over well with the authorities, so do a little research and get permission. If your friend has space on a private beach, this is the best way, because it's a long day and having access to a house is really clutch.

PREP TIME: 5–6 HOURS

COOK TIME: 1 HOUR

MEMORIES: FOREVER

YIELD: 20 SERVINGS

FOR THE TOOLS AND MATERIALS

12–15 people you like a lot; clam baking alone is a real downer

2 spade shovels

At least 40 softball-size rocks

Wood for the fire—lots of it, because you need the fire to be going for hours before you even cook anything

25–30 lb (11.4–13.7 kg) seaweed, preferably rockweed cut from nearby rocks (don't pull it off; use a knife)

A large canvas cover soaked in the ocean for a couple of hours

FOR THE FOOD

20 (1- to 2-lb [455- to 910-g]) lobsters

10 lb (4.6 kg) clams (I like cherrystones)

10 lb (4.6 kg) mussels

3 lb (1265 g) chorizo

20 ears fresh corn

3 lb (1365 g) small new potatoes, wrapped in foil (Hint: I like to parboil the potatoes for 15 minutes so they start to get a little tender and then finish them in the pit)

Infused Butter (page 49), melted, for serving

Purchase your seafood the day of and keep it cold. If you can't use a fridge, keep it in heavily iced coolers in the shade. Have beverages ready and begin drinking here.

You're going to need to dig a 3 x 3-foot (1 x 1-m) pit 2–3 feet (60–91 cm) deep. Line the bottom with the rocks and then pile the wood on top and light the fire. The fire needs to blaze for at least 3 hours. Feed the fire constantly to keep it burning hot. The rocks act as the roasting oven, so they need to be around 425°F (220°C).

Dig a small separate pit about 2 feet (60 cm) wide and 1 foot (30 cm) deep 8 feet (7.2 m) away from your main pit to put the extra ash in.

When the wood has burned down to white ash, shovel it off and place it in the separate pit you have dug and then place your first layer of seaweed on the hot coals. Cover it completely. Then add your seafood, chorizo, corn and potatoes right on top of the seaweed and cover it all with a second layer of seaweed and then the large soaked tarp. Continue drinking.

The cooking time will vary, but start checking it after an hour. The clams and mussels will have opened and the lobsters will be bright red in color. The chorizo, corn and potatoes will be ready when the lobster is cooked.

Have a table ready and put it all out to be consumed with some melted butter.

Enjoy the splendors of your victory.

FABULOUS FISH TACOS

Having lived in Cali, I've been served some remarkable fish tacos. One was even close to a perfect 10. So when I set out to make my own, I knew I had to up the ante. I wanted them to have a fresh, crunchy slaw and a tender, pan-seared, flaky fish and for it all to be served on a delicious homemade tortilla. Once you taste these, you will see fish tacos go to an 11.

CRUNCHY COLESLAW

Fish tacos need some tasty, crunchy slaw on top. This fits the bill and then some!

PREP TIME: 20 MINUTES

MARINATING TIME: 1 HOUR

MAKE THIS 2 HOURS BEFORE YOU MAKE THE FISH TACOS

YIELD: 6 SERVINGS

½ head green cabbage
1 large carrot
½ red onion, thinly sliced
1 tbsp (9 g) minced jalapeño
1 tbsp (15 ml) fresh lime juice
2 tbsp (30 ml) apple cider vinegar
¼ cup (56 g) Mayo That Rocks (page 26)
1 tsp (5 ml) honey
1 tsp (6 g) kosher salt
2 tbsp (6 g) chopped fresh cilantro

Using a box grater, shred the cabbage and carrot and place into a bowl. Add the onion and jalapeño and mix well. Combine the lime juice, cider vinegar, mayo, honey and salt in a separate bowl. Pour over the slaw mix, stir to combine and then let it sit for an hour for the flavors to meld. Mix in the cilantro and it's ready to go!

SPICED FLOUR TORTILLAS

Warm, soft and tender, these tortillas are amazing. Once you try these, you will never want the cardboard ones you get from the store. I use flour tortillas for everything: wraps, quesadillas, world peace. They're perfection when you toss on a little spice rub and bake them for homemade chips.

PREP TIME: 40 MINUTES

COOK TIME: 15–20 MINUTES TO MAKE ALL THE TORTILLAS

MAKE THESE WHILE THE COLESLAW AND FISH MARINATE

YIELD: 8 TORTILLAS

2 cups (240 g) all-purpose flour, plus more for dusting

1 tsp (6 g) salt

2 tsp (10 g) baking powder

2 tsp (6 g) chili powder

1 tsp (3 g) ground cumin

¼ cup (60 g) Cumin- and Annatto-Infused Lard of Love (page 179) or chilled shortening

½ cup (120 ml) Homemade Chicken Broth (page 174), more as needed

Combine the flour, salt, baking powder, chili powder and cumin in the bowl of a food processor. Put in the lard and process until completely cut in, about 30 seconds. It should hold its shape when you squeeze it in your hand. Add the chicken broth and process for 1 minute, until the dough forms a ball. If it does not form a ball, add 1 tablespoon (15 ml) more broth and process again, until the dough comes together.

Take it out and knead it for 1 minute on a lightly floured surface. Cover with a towel and let it rest for 20 minutes.

Cut the dough into 8 equal pieces and roll them into balls. Cover the balls with the towel. Using a rolling pin, roll the balls into 7- to 8-inch (18- to 20-cm) rounds. Place a nonstick griddle over medium heat. Do not add oil! Two at a time, gently lay the tortillas on the hot griddle for about a minute a side, until brown with tiny black spots. Remove and stack the tortillas, and cover with a new dry towel to keep them nice, warm and pliable.

(continued)

Flour tortillas in raw form.

Add baking powder to the flour and salt.

Add the chili powder.

Add the cumin.

Add the lard.

Add the broth.

Dough!

Knead it.

ce the dough into pieces.

Make a ball.

ɔll it out.

Griddle time!

FABULOUS FISH TACOS

Now this is a two-step process. First you want to marinate the fish, and while that's going you make the flour tortillas and then cook the fish. When you are done with all that, your coleslaw will be ready as well and it will be time to eat those righteous fish tacos, dude!

PREP TIME: 20 MINUTES

MARINATING TIME: 1 HOUR

COOK TIME: 8–10 MINUTES

REST TIME: 5 MINUTES

YIELD: 4 TACOS

FOR THE MARINADE

½ cup (120 ml) fresh-squeezed orange juice

3 tbsp (45 ml) lime juice

2 cloves garlic, smashed

1 tbsp (9 g) minced jalapeño

1 tsp (5 ml) honey

½ cup (24 g) chopped fresh cilantro

1 lb (455 g) fresh mahi-mahi, cut into 4 (4-oz [113-g]) pieces

FOR THE SPICE RUB

1 tbsp (9 g) chili powder

2 tsp (6 g) ground cumin

1 tsp (4 g) brown sugar

1 tsp (6 g) salt

Canola oil

1 recipe Spiced Flour Tortillas (page 159)

1 recipe Crunchy Coleslaw (page 158)

Chopped fresh cilantro, for serving

To make the marinade, combine all the ingredients in a bowl. Place the mahi-mahi in a zip-top bag and pour in the marinade. Squeeze out as much air as possible and place in the fridge for 1 hour.

Meanwhile, make the spice rub by combining all the ingredients in a bowl.

Now, go make the flour tortillas!

Take the fish out of the fridge and remove the fish from the marinade. Pat dry with paper towels. Sprinkle both sides with the spice rub. Let it stand for 10 minutes while you heat up a pan.

Place a cast-iron or nonstick pan over medium heat. Add a little canola oil and sear the fish, 4 minutes a side. Don't move the fish around; once you put it in the pan, don't touch it until you flip it. Remove it to a rack and let it rest for 5 minutes. Coarsely shred the fish and pile it on the tortillas, then top with the coleslaw and finish with a sprinkle of fresh cilantro.

TODAY'S
MENU
Chef Joe

IT'S TAMALE TIME

The first time I ever had the pleasure of tasting an authentic tamale was when I lived in LA. The experience of eating one made from scratch was an epiphany. The fluffy, moist masa gently enveloping the rich, tangy, slow-roasted pork was an amalgamation of flavors I had never encountered before. I was transported to Mexico. I was hooked. After my second bite I blankly stared at my wife, Carey. "Are you okay?" she quipped. Nothing. "Joe?" I finally spoke. "This is the most incredible thing I've ever tasted. I need to know how they did this." With those words my wife knew it was on. Big-time.

Once I dig into something I go all the way. I need to go to the bottom of the challenge and then dig even more. The research began. I poured over books and posts on the net about authentic tamales, reading every little tidbit I could. As I did, this one thing became very clear: masa was the key to it all. It was the Bobby Orr of the tamale. The linchpin. The cog that makes the world go round, and of course, it had to be made from scratch.

So that meant I needed to source some field dent corn. Typically, this is used as cattle feed. I know, strange but true. After a little legwork, I found some. Then came the stumper. Nixtamalization. Wow. I saw this word and my first thought was, "What the hell is that?! Maybe this is too much. Maybe I have finally bitten off more than I can chew ..." NO WAY! I'm not going out that easy. So I put on my big boy pants and stepped into the octagon. Ready for a fight. It was a great battle, but in the end I was triumphant! Now, making my own lard, chicken broth and whatever I wanted to put inside seemed like a snap. If I was going this far I knew that there was only one thing I could stuff them with: cochinita pibil, an amazing pork dish that I had come to worship. I was on my way to Mexico sans airfare. The tamale was coming....

TAMALES STUFFED WITH COCHINITA PIBIL

Rich, tender pork wrapped lovingly in a delicate blanket of corn masa and then steamed to perfection. Mixed with roasted corn salsa and a tangy from-scratch lime crema and it instantly rockets up the charts to #1.

LIME CREMA CREAMY GOODNESS

Crema is cool. It has a cool name, a cool look and a cool taste. Making it from scratch really ups its game as well, and it's only three ingredients! I don't like sour cream—it's too thick and gloppy—but I do love crema. I know it seems like the same thing, but it's not. It's smoother and beautifully subtle. Plus, you can add things to it and play with it. Fun and you get to ferment, what a day!

PREP TIME: 20 MINUTES

FERMENTATION TIME: 24 HOURS

MAKE THIS 3 DAYS BEFORE THE TAMALES

YIELD: 1 CUP (240 G)

1 cup (240 ml) heavy cream

1 tbsp (15 ml) buttermilk (with active cultures)

2 tbsp (30 ml) fresh lime juice

In a pot over medium heat, warm the heavy cream to between 90°F and 100° F (32°C and 38°C). Pour the heavy cream into a mason jar and add the buttermilk. Cover the jar with cheesecloth and set the lid on loosely. Fermentation is now ready to do its thing. Let it sit in a warm part of the kitchen for 24 hours. It will thicken and it will be awesome. Now remove the cheesecloth, stir in the lime juice, and it's ready to go. Put the lid on tight and keep it in the fridge for up to a week. Use it at will. Awesome for tacos, nachos and empanadas!

ACHIOTE POWDER

A classic Mexican rub from the Yucatan, achiote powder is deep, rich and earthy. It's the backbone of cochinita pibil. The base is the annatto seed, which is a natural coloring for some cheddar cheeses and rice dishes, and back in the day it was mixed with oil and used as a natural suntan lotion. What!!

PREP TIME: 10 MINUTES

MAKE THIS 3 DAYS BEFORE THE TAMALES

YIELD: 1 CUP (120 G)

¼ cup (20 g) annatto seeds
2 tbsp (12 g) cumin seeds
2 tsp (4 g) coriander seeds
2 tsp (4 g) black peppercorns
1 tbsp (4 g) red pepper flakes
½ stick Mexican Ceylon cinnamon
4 allspice berries
1 tbsp (3 g) Mexican oregano
2 arbol chiles, seeds removed
1 tbsp (18 g) kosher salt

Place the annatto in a spice grinder and take it for a whirl until it's a fine powder; place in a large bowl. Toast the cumin seeds, coriander and black peppercorns in a dry sauté pan over medium heat, moving them around constantly, and cook for 2 minutes. Transfer to the spice grinder and grind them until fine. Place them in the bowl. Grind all the rest and add them to the bowl. Mix until combined.

ACHIOTE PASTE

This is my take on the paste that is the key to cochinita pibil. It is typically done with sour oranges, but I use limes and oranges to create a similar flavor. The serrano gives it a really nice kick. Marinate anything you can think of with this. I brush it on fish when I'm grilling and it always makes people super happy.

PREP TIME: 15 MINUTES

MAKE THIS 3 DAYS BEFORE THE TAMALES

YIELD: 1 CUP (230 G)

1 cup (230 g) Achiote Powder (page 172)

1 serrano chile

10 cloves garlic

2 tbsp (6 g) chopped fresh cilantro

¼ cup (60 ml) fresh lime juice

1 cup (240 ml) fresh orange juice

1 tbsp (15 ml) apple cider vinegar

Place the achiote in a blender. Stem the serrano and place in the bender along with everything else. Blend all together until a loose marinade forms.

HOMEMADE CHICKEN BROTH

We need this homemade broth to bring our tamales to the next level. When I make this, I make a lot, because I use it for everything from soups to sauces; it gives anything you make a deeper, richer flavor. It's also a good way to use up veggies that are ready to turn. I make whole chickens all the time for dinner and just save the bones in my freezer until I'm ready to make some broth! I use my big tamale pot and make a ton. Then I freeze the rest in ½-gallon (1900-ml) portions so whenever my wife, Carey, or I need some—boom, it's right there!

PREP TIME: 25 MINUTES

COOK TIME: 5–6 HOURS

MAKE THIS 2 DAYS BEFORE CREATING THE TAMALES

YIELD: 2 GALLONS (7.2 L)

8 whole leftover roasted chicken carcasses

2 yellow onions, halved

10 cloves garlic, crushed

6 carrots, halved

6 celery sticks, halved

1 jalapeño, halved

1 bay leaf

2 tbsp (10 g) whole peppercorns

6 sprigs parsley

10 sprigs fresh thyme

4 sprigs fresh oregano

3 gallons (11.4 L) cold water

Place all the ingredients in a large pot and pour in the water. It should cover everything. Bring it all to *almost* a boil. Do not let it boil or it will get cloudy. Turn it down to a simmer for 5–6 hours. No stirring. When it's done, remove it from the heat and let it cool, skimming off anything that's collected on top. When it's finished cooling, store it in portions. It will stay fresh for a week in the fridge and 6 months in the freezer.

FROM-SCRATCH MASA

I know this seems a little crazy, but the first time I made this and tasted the tamale with from-scratch masa, I was literally transported to Mexico. You can taste the love. You need to use field dent corn here, not sweet corn or popcorn. Field dent corn is typically used for cattle feed, so it's easy to find. We are going to put it through nixtamalization. The Aztec first created this process—they knew what they were doing! It's harder to say that word than it is to do the process, trust me. We are just adding the dried corn to a solution of water and slaked lime. What does this do? A couple of things: it's going to grind way easier, the flavor is going to be crazy good and it releases niacin, which is really good for you! Once the corn does its thing in the solution, it's then called nixtamal, and you are ready to make the masa for our killer tamales just using a food processor! You can find the corn and slaked lime on Amazon.

PREP TIME: 15 MINUTES

STEEP, SOAK AND RINSE TIME: 2 HOURS 45 MINUTES

COOK TIME: 12–15 MINUTES

MAKE THIS 2 DAYS BEFORE YOU MAKE THE TAMALES

YIELD: 4½ POUNDS (2050 G)

3 lb (1350 g) dried field dent corn

1 gallon (3.8 L) water

¼ cup (60 ml) slaked lime (calcium hydroxide)

Spread your corn out and make sure there are no offensive specks, rocks, bugs or rotten kernels. In an 8-quart (7.2-L) nonreactive pot over high heat, heat the water and slaked lime until the slaked lime is dissolved; the solution will still be cloudy. Once that happens, add the field dent corn and bring it to a boil. Let it boil for 15 minutes and then remove it from the heat and let it steep, lid on, for 2 hours.

Now pour the corn into a large colander. Then put it into a large bowl filled with warm water. Let it soak for 15 minutes, stirring it to make sure all the slaked lime is coming off. Drain into the colander and place it back into the bowl, fill with warm water again and rinse it really well, moving it around. Repeat this until the water is clear and no scum rises to the top. You have to get ALL the slaked lime off. It will not taste good.

Now to make masa is very simple. Just grind it in small batches of 2 cups (480 g) in the food processor, running the food processor and scraping down the sides and then running it again until it's the right consistency, an evenly ground, soft cornmeal-like texture. Each batch should take about 1 minute and 15 seconds to process. Store it in the fridge overnight. It will keep in the fridge for a week and in the freezer for 6 months.

COCHINITA PIBIL

I discovered and fell in love with this traditional dish from the Yucatan when I was living in LA. Pork is slathered in an earthy, citrusy achiote paste and then wrapped in banana leaves and slow roasted until it's pull-apart tender. The first time I tasted it I felt transported back generations. It felt so simple and complex at the same time. It warmed my soul and gratified my belly. I was infatuated. I use this in my tamales because this plus tamales equals insane yumminess.

PREP TIME: 20 MINUTES, PLUS OVERNIGHT MARINATING TIME

COOK TIME: 6–6½ HOURS

MAKE THIS 2 DAYS BEFORE THE TAMALES

YIELD: 1½ QUARTS (840 G)

4 lb (1800 g) boneless pork butt (shoulder)

1½ tsp (9 g) kosher salt

20 cloves garlic, divided

1 cup (230 g) Achiote Paste (page 173)

2 fresh or frozen and thawed banana leaves, cut crosswise in half

1 white onion, chopped

2 serrano peppers, seeded and chopped

1–1½ cups (240–360 ml) Homemade Chicken Broth (page 174)

1 orange, cut in half

Place the pork on a clean cutting board and pierce fifteen 2-inch (5-cm) deep holes evenly over the top of the shoulder. Rub the salt all over the surface of the pork. Insert 15 of the whole garlic cloves into the holes. Wearing a pair of gloves because the achiote paste stains, rub the paste all over the meat. Place it in a covered container and refrigerate overnight.

Layer a 6-quart (5.4-L) slow cooker with the thawed banana leaves. Tuck 2 overlapping pieces into the pot with the ends facing you. Place the last piece of banana leaf across the others (handle to handle), and tuck it in so all the leaves are flat against the inner surface of the pot, with the ends hanging out. Spread the remaining 5 garlic cloves, half of the chopped white onion and half of the serranos on top of the banana leaves. Place the pork on top of the onions and pour the chicken broth around it. Top with the remaining onion and serranos. Squeeze the orange halves over the top, and tuck the halves around the pork. Fold the ends of the banana leaves up and over the meat, tucking them neatly inside. Place the last banana leaf half crosswise over the top, tuck in the ends, and close the lid. Place the slow cooker on high for 6–6½ hours.

When it's done, the pork should be tender and pull apart. Let the meat rest in the sauce until it's cool enough to handle, then coarsely shred it and moisten with the sauce. Stuff it in tortillas, use it for a killer quesadilla or do what I love to do and stuff it in the ultimate tamale! You can store this in the fridge overnight.

CUMIN- AND ANNATTO-INFUSED LARD OF LOVE

Lard has a bad reputation, but it's slander. Personally, I think its name has a lot to do with it. If it were called, say, "Snowy Love" or "White Butter," everyone would use it. It's actually good for you and it's natural. Lard rules. That's right, I said it. Lard rules. What, you disagree? Well, it's amazing for baked goods; biscuits and pie crusts are ridiculously flaky and tender using lard. Frying with lard? Three words: crispy, crispy and crispy. Rich, addicting traditional tamales were not made with shortening. So right there is the end game for me. I've made tamales with shortening and there is no comparison. We are already making the masa and its best friend is lard, so let's make sure they get to party together. I infuse it with some earthy flavors to up the game even more. Wait until you see the cool auburn hue it has. Now, since this is for tamales, we are using back fat, which is richer; if you were going to do a lot of baking with this, I would suggest not infusing it and using leaf lard, which comes from around the kidneys and has a cleaner flavor.

PREP TIME: 45 MINUTES

COOK TIME: 1–1½ HOURS

MAKE THIS 1 DAY BEFORE THE TAMALES

YIELD: 2 CUPS (450 G)

3 lb (1350 g) back fat
¼ cup (60 ml) water
2 tbsp (12 g) annatto seeds
1 tbsp (6 g) cumin seeds

Place the back fat into the freezer for ½ hour. It makes it easier to slice. Remove it and chop it into 1-inch (2.5-cm) chunks. In a large Dutch oven over medium heat, add the water; this helps stop the fat from scorching. Add the fat, annatto seeds and cumin seeds and stir occasionally. About an hour later, the water will be gone and your fat will be rendering. Stir again, and after a little bit there will be brown bits floating their way to the surface; these are cracklings. Capture them and put them on paper towels. More on those later. Keep stirring and you will notice all the fat has rendered and the rest of the cracklings are on the bottom. Turn off the heat. Line a colander with cheesecloth, place on top of a large bowl and strain; let it cool for 30 minutes. I find it's easier to handle. Keep the cracklings to the side and pour the golden liquid love into mason jars. Let it cool to room temperature and place it in the fridge. It will keep for 3–4 months in the fridge. Lightly season the cracklings with any kind of rub or even just salt and grab a beer. What happens after that is up you.

(continued)

Fat back.

Begin to render.

Rendering!

Strain.

BLACK BEAN AND ROASTED CORN SALSA

Fresh salsa is so delicious and easy. This one is so good you'll be making it all the time. A hint of sweetness from the roasted corn, deep richness of roasted garlic and the perfect amount of heat from the spicy serrano—it's great on a chip, in a wrap or stuffed in a tamale!

PREP TIME: 20 MINUTES

MAKE THIS THE DAY OF THE TAMALES

YIELD: 2 CUPS (480 G)

3 ears fresh corn, shucked, silk removed

2 cloves garlic, in skin

2 cups (500 g) black beans, drained and rinsed

1 red onion, diced

2 tbsp (30 ml) lime juice

1 serrano, minced

1 tsp (3 g) chili powder

1 tsp (3 g) ground cumin

1 tsp (6 g) kosher salt

Grill the corn until it's lightly charred and brown on all sides. When they have cooled a tad, remove the kernels with a knife into a bowl. Place a small, dry skillet over medium heat, add the garlic cloves and turn until the skin is charred on all sides. Remove, let cool, then peel the charred skin off and mince. Add the black beans, onion, garlic, lime juice, serrano, chili powder, cumin and salt to the bowl with the charred corn. Stir to combine. Now grabs some chips or stuff some tamales: you have amazing salsa!

TAMALES STUFFED WITH COCHINITA PIBIL

Here it is: the pièce de résistance. I fell in love with these wondrous culinary masterpieces in LA and never looked back. These take a bit of time, but they are oh so worth it.

PREP TIME: 1 HOUR

SOAKING TIME: 2 HOURS

COOK TIME: 1 HOUR AND 45 MINUTES

ENJOYMENT TIME: ETERNAL

YIELD: 25 TAMALES

1 (6-oz [170-g]) package dried cornhusks

12 oz (340 g) Cumin- and Annatto-Infused Lard of Love (page 179)

2 tbsp (28 g) Infused Butter (page 49)

5 cups (800 g) From-Scratch Masa (page 175)

1 tsp (6 g) salt

2 tsp (10 g) baking powder

2 cups (470 ml) Homemade Chicken Broth (page 174)

3 cups (700 g) Cochinita Pibil (page 177), slightly warmed

2 cups (480 g) Black Bean and Roasted Corn Salsa (page 182), divided

Kitchen twine

1 recipe Lime Crema Creamy Goodness (page 170)

First things first. We need to get the husks flexible and to do that all we need to do is soak them in hot water. So grab a large bowl and place the husks in, cover them with hot water and put something heavy on them to keep them from floating. Give them 2 hours and they will be perfect. So take that into consideration when starting this tamale-making adventure.

In a small saucepan over medium-low heat, melt the lard and butter together and keep warm. In the bowl of a stand mixer fitted with the paddle attachment, combine the masa, salt and baking powder. Slowly add the lard/butter combo until fully incorporated. The dough should be moist but not wet and runny. If it is too wet, add a little more masa. Gradually add the broth until moist like a batter. Place it in the fridge.

Take the husks out of the water and squeeze out the excess water; remove the silk as well. They should be moist and flexible. Mix the cochinita and 1 cup (240 g) of the salsa in a bowl and set aside. Cut the kitchen twine into thirty 12-inch (30-cm) pieces. Remove the tamale dough from the fridge.

Lay one corn husk on your work surface, curled-side up. Spread ¼–½ cup (60–120 g) of masa in the center of the husk, and use the back of a spoon to spread it into a roughly 5- to 6-inch (12.5- to 15-cm)circle. Now place 2 tablespoons (30 g) of the filling down the center of the dough. Lift the long sides of the husk so the masa encloses the filling, then open it flat again. Fold the pointed end in to cover the filling halfway; leave the opposite end open. Fold one long side snugly over the masa, rolling it up to enclose the filling. Tie with the string right around the middle. Repeat with the remaining ingredients.

(continued)

Spread out the masa.

Mix Cochinita Pibil with the salsa.

Lay in the center.

Getting ready to steam.

TAMALES STUFFED WITH COCHINITA PIBIL (CONTINUED)

On to steaming! I use my large tamale steamer over medium-high heat. You can use a large lidded pot with a colander or metal strainer. Place the tamales into the steamer folded-side down. Put the lid on and steam for an hour and a half. Pour in more hot water when it gets low: don't let it boil away! After an hour and a half take them off the heat and let the tamales sit in the steamer, lid on, for 15 minutes. Now take them out. The dough should be firm and tender. If the masa sticks to the husk, they are not done. Steam another 15 minutes and check again. When they are ready, remove and place on a plate and open. You will be amazed at the aromas. Serve with the remaining 1 cup (240 g) salsa and crema if you want or leave it naked and dig in!

from scratch
Chef Joe Gatt
HILLROCK

GOIN' HOG WILD

There is nothing that tastes and smells as marvelous as a whole roasted pig. This kind of event is as memorable as it gets. Your friends and family, beverages in hand, will marvel at the remarkable pig slowly spinning on the spit for hours, the skin gradually deepening to a dark mahogany as the fat drips and kisses the charcoal with a sizzle. It is a mesmerizing scene, to say the least. They will horde around as it comes off the fire. The crispy skin will crackle as you begin to pull all the luscious pork. Hands will shoot in from everywhere just to get a taste. A morsel. They will all be clamoring for a plate of the glistening pork goodness. Their patience will be rewarded as they have their first taste of that succulent, juicy and oh-so-savory meat. Heaven.

Cooking a whole hog was something I wanted to do for such a long time, but I was always the bridesmaid and never the bride. I mean, it was always fantastic to attend a pig roast, but I wanted to do one of my own. My birthday seemed like the perfect opportunity for it, and we needed to roast a pig for the show. So calls where placed, a pig was found, a fire was lit, beers were consumed, much pork was eaten and great times were had by all. It's a little bit of work, but it's a blast to do with friends and it really is spectacular.

WHOLE HOG

I love whole hog. I mean, what's not to love? Lots of delicious pork and sauces, plus all the yummy side dishes like my masa cornbread—and the best part is you need to invite tons of people and they bring booze. Sounds like a great way to spend the day!

ROCK STAR BBQ RUB

Spicy, sweet and complex (kind of like me!), this BBQ rub finds its way into many of my creations. It's not just for pork and chicken. I use it on fish, in sauces, sprinkled on my homemade tortilla chips. It's really cool how you can use it for anything. I have worked on this recipe for years. I really love it and I think you will, too. It has quite a few spices in it, so I suggest that you make a double or triple batch and store it in mason jars for the future. It will go quicker than you think.

PREP TIME: 15 MINUTES

MAKE THIS 1 WEEK BEFORE THE PIG ROAST

YIELD: 1½ CUPS (180 G)

1 cup (180 g) dark brown sugar
2 tbsp (36 g) kosher salt
2 tbsp (12 g) chipotle powder
1 tbsp (6 g) smoked paprika
1 tbsp (6 g) fresh cracked black pepper
1 tbsp (5 g) cayenne pepper
1 tbsp (6 g) garlic powder
1 tbsp (6 g) onion powder
1 tbsp (6 g) toasted and ground cumin
1 tbsp (3 g) dried oregano
1 tbsp (3 g) dried thyme
2 tsp (4 g) dry mustard powder
2 tsp (4 g) ground coriander
2 tsp (4 g) ground allspice
2 tsp (4 g) espresso
1 tsp (5 g) baking cocoa
1 tsp (1 g) dried orange peel
1 tsp (1 g) jalapeño powder
1 tsp (1 g) ginger powder

Mix all the ingredients in a bowl and store in mason jars.

NORTH CAROLINA SAUCE GATTO STYLE

This is my version of my favorite of all the BBQ sauces. I love the tangy vinegar base with that hit of heat. I feel it complements the whole or any prep of the pig to "porkfection."

PREP TIME: 20 MINUTES

MAKE THIS 2 DAYS BEFORE THE PIG ROAST

YIELD: 2 CUPS (480 G)

1 cup (240 ml) cider vinegar

2 tbsp (30 g) Killer Ketchup (page 22)

1 tbsp (12 g) brown sugar

1 tbsp (15 ml) fresh lemon juice

½ tbsp (9 g) kosher salt

1 tsp (5 ml) Worcestershire sauce

1 tsp (2 g) cayenne pepper

1 tsp (2 g) smoked paprika

1 tsp (2 g) dry mustard powder

1 tsp (3 g) fresh cracked pepper

1 tsp (1 g) red pepper flakes

In a mason jar, combine the vinegar, ketchup, brown sugar and lemon juice; screw the lid on and shake well until the sugar is dissolved. Add the remaining ingredients and shake away. Throw it in the fridge for a couple of hours to let the flavors meld and become friends.

PICKLED WATERMELON RINDS

A southern BBQ staple. These crispy, tart, sweet bites of love are perfect with the whole hog. People will marvel at the color and taste of this super unique side dish.

PREP TIME: 20 MINUTES

COOK TIME: 20 MINUTES

MAKE THESE 2 DAYS BEFORE THE PIG ROAST

YIELD: TWO 16-OUNCE (450-G) JARS

2 lb (900 g) peeled watermelon rind

1 tbsp (18 g) kosher salt

3 cups (600 g) sugar

1½ cups (350 ml) apple cider vinegar

½ cup (120 ml) white vinegar

1 whole clove

6 whole black peppercorns

1 tsp (5 g) Pickling Spice (page 43)

1 tsp (3 g) ground ginger

1 cinnamon stick

2 (16-oz [450-g]) mason jars

Cut the rind into 2 x 2-inch (5 x 5-cm) pieces. Fill a large pot with water, add the salt and bring to a boil. Place the rinds in and cook until they are tender, 10–15 minutes. Drain the rinds in a large colander. Divide them between the mason jars, packing them until they are 2 inches (5 cm) from the top. Combine all the remaining ingredients in the pot, bring to a boil and boil for 3 minutes. Remove the cinnamon stick and carefully pour the hot liquid over the rinds in the mason jars. Screw the lids on and let them sit on the counter until they are at room temperature, then pop them in the fridge to sit overnight. They will last in the fridge for 2–3 weeks.

BODACIOUS BLUEBERRY CHIPOTLE BBQ SAUCE

My in-laws, Ben and Sharon, are from Maine. When we visit during the summer, fresh blueberries are everywhere. Well, I love me some sweet and spicy BBQ sauce, so when I wanted some spiciness, my first thought was chipotle, the perfect complement to the blueberry. I gave it a try, and damn! Perfect for the whole hog! This is also rocking on grilled chicken.

COOK TIME: 20 MINUTES

MAKE THIS 1 DAY BEFORE THE PIG ROAST

YIELD: 2 CUPS (480 G)

1 tbsp (15 ml) canola oil
3 cloves garlic, minced
2 tsp (4 g) fresh ginger, minced
2 tbsp (30 g) minced chipotles in adobo
2 cups (300 g) fresh blueberries
½ cup (120 g) Killer Ketchup (page 22)
⅓ cup (80 ml) cider vinegar
2 tbsp (24 g) brown sugar
1 tbsp (15 ml) molasses
⅛ tsp ground allspice
1 tsp (6 g) kosher salt
2 tbsp (30 ml) fresh lemon juice

Heat the canola in a Dutch oven over medium heat. Add the garlic, ginger and chipotles and cook, stirring, for 1 minute. Add the blueberries, ketchup, vinegar, brown sugar, molasses, allspice and salt and stir for 1 minute to combine thoroughly. Lower the heat and bring the sauce to a simmer. Cook for 15 minutes, stirring every couple of minutes. The pectin in the blueberries will release and naturally thicken it. Take it off the heat and stir in the lemon juice, grab your immersion blender and puree until it's smooth and you are good to go!

ROASTED CHILE AND MASA SKILLET CORNBREAD

Cornbread is a staple at any great BBQ, but sometimes I feel it's a forgotten side dish, neglected and not cared for, and I didn't want to be Mommy Dearest, so I needed to make a cornbread with love and care. This is it, and the minute you have a bite, you will feel me hugging you. Now make it before I have to get my wire hanger!

PREP TIME: 25 MINUTES

COOK TIME: 30 MINUTES

MAKE THIS THE DAY OF THE PIG ROAST

YIELD: TWENTY 2-INCH (5-CM) PIECES

1 poblano pepper, halved lengthwise and seeded

1 serrano pepper, halved lengthwise and seeded

2 cups (320 g) From-Scratch Masa (page 175)

1 cup (120 g) all-purpose flour

¼ cup (45 g) packed light brown sugar

2 tsp (10 g) baking powder

½ tsp baking soda

½ tsp kosher salt

2 eggs

½ cup (120 ml) buttermilk

½ cup (120 ml) whole milk

4 oz (120 g) Infused Butter (page 49), melted

Set your oven to broil. Adjust the oven rack to the top position. Line a baking sheet with foil and spray with nonstick spray. Place the peppers on the prepared baking sheet, skin side up, and roast them for 4–6 minutes, until the skin blisters and begins to char. Remove from the oven, let them cool for 2 minutes, place them in a plastic bag and seal it. Let them sit for 15 minutes, then take them out and peel the skins off. Then mince them.

Preheat your oven to 375°F (190°C, or gas mark 5). Butter a 12-inch (30-cm) cast-iron skillet. Thoroughly whisk together the masa, flour, brown sugar, baking powder, baking soda and salt in a large bowl. In a separate bowl, whisk together the eggs, buttermilk, milk and butter. Add the egg mixture and chiles to the dry mixture and stir until just combined. Do not overmix. Pour into the skillet and spread it out evenly. Bake for 25–30 minutes. Insert a paring knife into the center: if it comes out clean, your cornbread is perfect. Let it cool for 10 minutes, then slice and serve it up!

SPIT ROASTING A WHOLE HOG

There are tons of different ways to cook a whole hog—burying it with lava rocks wrapped in banana leaves (Hawaiian style), in a Caja China (traditional Cuban pig roaster box)—but the way I do it here is classic Americana: the spit roast. Now let's go release our inner Cro-Magnon man!

PREP TIME: 1 HOUR

COOK TIME: 6–8 HOURS FOR A 50- TO 60-POUND (22.8- TO 27.3-KG) PIG

FOR THE TOOLS AND MATERIALS

A rotisserie with an electric spit

60 lb (27.3 kg) charcoal (I prefer a 50/50 briquette and lump mix; see page 18)

A rake for moving coals

Stainless steel picture-hanging wire

Digital meat thermometer

Heatproof gloves

A knife and cleaver

Lots of beer

FOR THE FOOD

A locally raised fresh pig between 50 and 60 lb (22.8 to 27.3 kg) (order at least 2 weeks in advance)

2 recipes Rock Star BBQ Rub (page 192)

6 recipes Bodacious Beer Hamburger Buns (page 30)

2 recipes North Carolina Sauce Gatto Style (page 193)

2 recipes Bodacious Blueberry Chipotle BBQ Sauce (page 195)

6 recipes Spiced Flour Tortillas (page 159)

4 recipes Roasted Chile and Masa Skillet Cornbread (page 197)

2 recipes Pickled Watermelon Rinds (page 194)

The first thing you need to do is order a quality pig, between 50 and 60 pounds (22.8 to 27.3 kg), which will feed around 30 hungry guests and cook in 6–8 hours. Talk to your local butcher in advance to make sure they can get you one. If not, the Internet is always a handy tool for landing a pig; just make sure it was well raised and it's from a trusted source. Make sure that it comes cleaned and prepped. You don't want to have to do that part. If you need to get it the day before and you don't have a huge walk-in cooler at the house, you can store it wrapped in plastic in the bathtub covered in ice. This really works! Be sure to inform the household that you have done this.

Next step, secure a rotisserie. I say rent an electric-powered one. There are plenty of places to do that. Some pig-roasting professional caterers will rent you the equipment and bring the pig for you. Look into it. You can also build the pit from cinder blocks—it's not that hard, but it is very time-consuming, and if it's your first time doing this, renting an electric one will make the process much smoother. I love the classic spit in the middle of the yard slowly turning. It makes me happy.

Okay, it's roasting day. How exciting! The first thing you want to do is get your fire lit. I like to have a mixture of lump charcoal and briquettes. That way it stays hot but I still get that flavor from the lump. You're going to need about 60 pounds (27.3 kg) of charcoal (I just go with a pound [455 g] of charcoal per pound [455 g] of pig). Have an extra bag around just in case. You need the coals burning for a while before you start the pig. It's best to have another bucket of lit coals to use as you go. That way you are not adding unlit coals to the fire. It will keep a constant temperature and will make for more uniform cooking. Also, make sure the coals are spread out evenly. Use your handy rake to move the coals around to accomplish this.

You want your fire between 225°F and 250°F (105°C and 120°C). I found that if you can maintain the temperature at 250°F (120°C), the pig will cook at about 1 hour per 10 pounds (4500 g), but there are some factors that could influence that, such as wind, rain and the temperature outside, so use that as a loose guide. The pig itself needs to end up at 160°F (71°C) internal temperature. The USDA says you can do pork to 145°F (63°C), but I feel when doing a whole hog 155°F (68°C) is your best bet to be safe and still have it nice and moist. Once you take it off it will continue to cook a little. I think this temperature really works well.

Okay, back to the star of the day, the pig—you can season it however you like. Some people go sans rubs and just use salt to preserve the flavor. I like to use my rub and liberally sprinkle it all over the inner cavity. I then sprinkle some on the skin as well. Again, this is what I like to do; if you want your pig naked, rock on!

Once it's seasoned you need to get it onto the spit. This part can get tricky and having a couple of able-bodied people who aren't afraid to get their hands dirty would be helpful. You need to get the spit straight through the center of the pig from the mouth through the back end following the spine. Once you do that, tie the pig's feet tightly to the bottom bar with wire. Now you need to secure the body onto the spit with the wire so it doesn't move around while it's cooking. Fasten it tightly. This is essential. If it moves around, the pig will not cook evenly. The spit will have prong attachments to secure each end after the spit goes through. Thread those onto the spit and pierce them deep into the flesh. When we did it we also used what's called a U-bolt, which attaches the spine to the spit directly. It was helpful in securing the animal but not completely necessary if you have secured it well with the wire.

It's time for the pig to meet Mr. Fire. Let's get this party started. You're going to need two people to place it on the pit. Once it's on there, it's just a matter of time. This is one of the best parts. Now you hang out for 6–8 hours and talk about how awesome this is going to taste. Be sure to keep the fire evenly lit with coals. Toward the end of cooking, be checking the temperature in different parts of the animal with the digital thermometer. Again, I like to take it off at 155°F (68°C).

Once you hit the desired temperature, place the cooked pig on a long sturdy table, cover it with aluminum foil and let it rest for 30 minutes. The juices will redistribute and it will be much better. Once it's rested, get ready to serve. Tear off the skin and hit it with a little of the rub and serve it up. People will go crazy for it. Then, pull the pork, slice the tenderloin and place it into large containers. Don't forget the cheek meat! That, to me, is the best. Place the burger buns and the sauces out so people can make pulled pork sandwiches. I like putting out some homemade tortillas for people to use. Don't forget to put out all your sides: the cornbread and pickled watermelon rinds. Now people can grab some luscious pork and chow down. Sit back and soak in the praise. You did it! A whole hog!

ACKNOWLEDGMENTS

Well, the journey of writing this book has been exciting, fun, crazy and immensely rewarding. The number of people I have met who helped me get here would need its own book. With that said, I'd like to thank some people!

First and foremost, I'd like to thank my wife, Carey, for her undying support and belief in me. You are always there to lend a hand or a shoulder, depending on the situation. Thanks, babe—you are forever my partner in crime.

To my two children, Benjamin and Cassidy: you guys rock. I love you, you make me laugh until I cry and you are the best sous chefs ever. You both make life a wonderful place and I treasure every moment I have with you. You are my heart and soul.

Thanks to my mom, Lorraine: you are my inspiration in the kitchen and my rock in life. I would not be the person I am without your guidance and love.

To my best bud, Matt Mead: thanks for always believing, making me laugh and saying "bada-bing." You always say that!

Thanks to Uncle Ken and Auntie Paula for introducing me to true Mexican food when I was a teenager visiting you in Chicago. It woke up my taste buds and helped send me down the path I'm on.

Thanks to my producer Ryan, "Kav," for always being down to drive each other artistically and never being satisfied. "This is nothing!"

Thanks to the team at Page Street Publishing—Will, Marissa and Karen. You showed faith, and that will never be forgotten.

A huge thanks to everyone who helped me make my show *From Scratch*, especially Carey, the best producer/wife combo ever; thanks for rocking the chalk. My eternal friend, softball champion and fellow deviant, Tony Flanagan. Multifaceted cameraman, Adam Mikaelian. Big salami! Juice glass! My #1 go-getter and lobster wrangler, Emmy Fay. He might be in jail when he reads this, but I still love him: Shane Bronson. Todd "Tamworth" Gorell, for always making me and everyone else laugh. The preeminent personal assistant ever created, Emily Corwin. Photographer extraordinaire Kate Doherty. Phill Gelinas, you rock at making meat tubes and music. Chelsea, for always being in fifth gear and always bringing Phill. Jonah Kan, my right hand: I love when you are wrong (which is very rare)! Florence, for always letting us have the studio, and my investors, for making my dreams come true.

Thanks to my friend Andy Husbands, for helping me without hesitation.

Thanks to my boys in the WFM Woburn meat department for my nickname, "Spicy Joe Crazy Pants."

Thanks to my go-to recipe tester, Nancy Boyce. You are amazing.

Thanks to my recipe testers: Chris Mead, Aaron Lashua, Emily Goodberg, Jonah Kan, Karen Tracy, Leah Ashley and Mickey Palone, Marco Albano, Matty Mead, Nancy Osmer, Nancy Seglin, Phill Gelinas, Sharon Zolper, Carey Gatto and last but not least David and Leslie Wilson of the Bacon Tree in Winterport, Maine—delicious food and awesome people.

A big thank-you to my bro Ken Goodman, for making the food and me shine in every pic: you are a rock star.

Thank you to all the farmers, artisans and purveyors out there who make this world go 'round.

Chef Joe Gatto

ABOUT THE AUTHOR

If you are picking this book up, you should know that Chef Joe Gatto is a little outrageous and a ton of fun. So is this book. His path to writing this book and making food from scratch is unique and entertaining. Chef Joe is a private chef and culinary instructor and the host of the cutting-edge cooking show *From Scratch*. Joe has been cooking from scratch his whole life. Growing up on the counter of his mom's kitchen, stirring, sifting and chopping, he understood why the kitchen is truly the heart of the house. Joe was an independent filmmaker throughout his twenties and early thirties, making award-winning feature-length and short films. When his son, Benjamin, was born, he decided to pursue his lifelong passion: food. He began teaching first from his home, then professionally. He then was hired as a private chef and has many clients for whom he prepares all their meals each week. In 2013 his worlds collided when he created the show *From Scratch*. Wanting to teach people how he taught himself, breaking food down to its core, Chef Joe realized this was a natural evolution of his path. Combining his skill as a teacher, passion for scratch cooking and knowledge of film, he has created the most unique cooking show out there. He loves to show off local purveyors, farmers and artisans. Chef Joe works continuously with the community as well, teaching children and the underprivileged how to cook healthy and from scratch. He lives in Massachusetts and loves it (yes, the snow, too!). He has a gorgeous wife, Carey, who rocks his world, and two children, Benjamin and Cassidy, who are the peanut butter to his jelly.

INDEX

D

F

R

S